THE
FRAGILE
DEMOCRACY

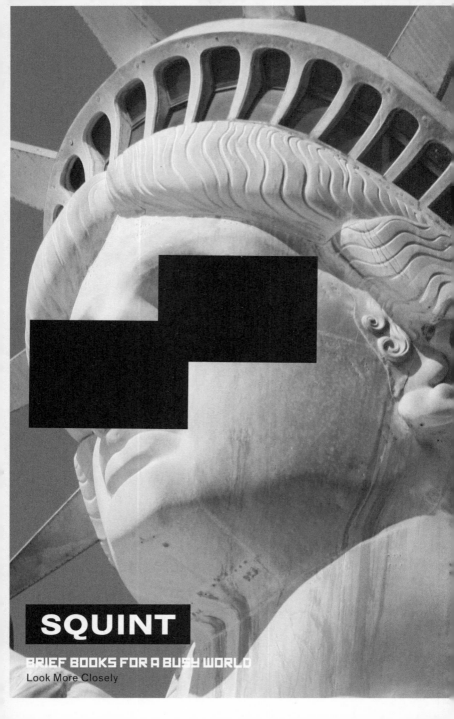

SQUINT

BRIEF BOOKS FOR A BUSY WORLD

Look More Closely

THE FRAGILE DEMOCRACY

THE RACE FOR THE US PRESIDENCY IN 2016

CHRISTOPHER JACKSON

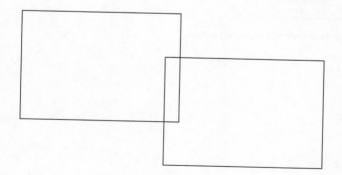

EYEWEAR PUBLISHING

First published in 2016
by Eyewear Publishing Ltd
Suite 333, 19-21 Crawford Street
Marylebone, London W1H 1PJ
United Kingdom

Typeset with graphic design by Edwin Smet
Printed in England by T J International Ltd, Padstow, Cornwall

The right of Christopher Jackson to be identified as author of
this work has been asserted in accordance with section 77
of the Copyright, Designs and Patents Act 1988

ISBN 978-1-911335-23-8

Eyewear wishes to thank Jonathan Wonham for
his generous patronage of our press.

WWW.EYEWEARPUBLISHING.COM

To my father,

It's not yet clear who shall be the next President of the United States but Guildford has its mayor.

CONTENTS

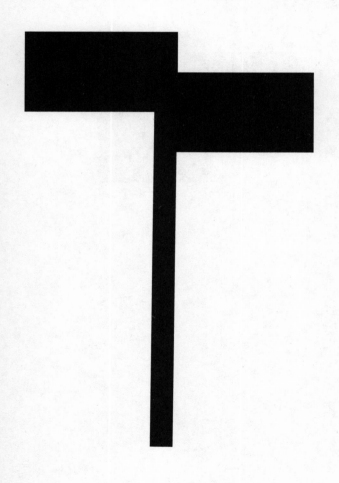

AUTHOR'S NOTE

Pity the man who writes a book about unfolding events. Perhaps only by trying to capture politics in a text like this can one begin to understand how subtly, and how quickly, things move. My first draft in February was full of qualifiers about the Trump candidacy. I, too, expected him to implode somehow. By March, I was removing references to the comparatively mild atmosphere on the Democrats' side. Summaries of policy positions quickly dated – first as Donald Trump, in his inimitable way, began to contradict himself with cheerful abandon, then as Hillary Clinton began to adopt some of Bernie Sanders' positions. The American political process, in its tumult and with its short attention span, is a moving target: at times, capturing it has been like trying to shoot a lion with a water-pistol.

But there were some things that were never going to change, and haven't changed. The Republican Party was never, for instance, going to suddenly embrace climate change or the nuclear agreement with Iran. Its candidates were never going to have a civil word to say about President Barack Obama. Hillary Clinton was unlikely ever to win over the young – at least in the context of a primary against Bernie Sanders. Sanders' candidacy – at time of writing, mathematically dead – will stand forever as the moment when a candidate presented arguments to the American people in favour of significant tax raises, and not only evaded ridicule, but found himself adored for it. We now face the strange possibility that a 73-year-old democratic socialist with a patchy record on gun control might symbolise the future of America: out of all the candidates in the race, his is the constituency that is expanding. The process shall only get noisier, and more complex, from here: America is like some vast orchestra which doesn't yet know what music is in front of it. The Hillary Clinton e-mail scandal, vice-presidential picks, terror attacks, financial shocks, 'gaffes' in the debates – all these things may yet have their impact. Politics is the unforeseen. Any cut-off in the great stream of events is essentially arbitrary.

And yet America, in all its gigantism and noise, complexity and even madness, demands to be written about not just in retrospect, but in real time. Five months ago, there were moments when I thought Donald Trump might have found a novel way for a billionaire to bring on personal bankruptcy. Now, a small but noticeably growing part of me thinks he might be the next President of the United States. He has bewitched and infuriated the world – often he has caused those emotions in people simultaneously. He has created a climate of unreality in which one wonders whether amusement, as opposed to disgust, might not be the appropriate response. In an interview with *The Daily Beast*, the comedian Ricky Gervais was relaxed about the prospect of a Trump presidency: 'If he gets in, I don't want him to be a good president. I want him to be a funny but terrible president. Because nothing will really happen, let's face it.'[1]

Possibly nothing too bad would happen to Ricky Gervais. But Gervais' attitude shows how far apparently intelligent people have bought into the world which Trump, aided and abetted by the media, has created. Facts don't matter – isn't life really just some vast form of entertainment?

We may have forgotten during these last years of Republican obstructionism (outlined in Chapter Two) throughout which false claims have often been peddled about Obama's 'weakness' – that the presidency is not, as

Gervais seems to think, a symbolic position. One can see where the confusion has arisen. It is *partly* symbolic. George Washington is on your dollar bill, and three of his successors stare down from Mount Rushmore. But it remains also an office of immense power – particularly if, as would likely be the case in the event of a Trump administration, Congress isn't inclined to obstruct the president's agenda. Even the least consequential American president changes the world. It will be argued that Obama's method of governing has been largely intelligent. Difficult situations were weighed; solutions – some successful, some not – were put forward (see Chapters Three and Four). It was a fundamentally benign project. Where he has had setbacks – in Libya or arguably on international trade – it has always been a symptom of departure from those stated principles. Whereas his successes were due to those principles – to a commitment to reasoned analysis.

This book explains how our dislocation from reality came about. It seeks to bring us back down to earth with some simple propositions, and contends that some things are eternally true: order is better than chaos; kindness is superior to violence; inclusiveness is good and extremism tedious; and it is a sensible idea to conserve our planet. Though this election, in all its glitz and controversy, can sometimes suggest otherwise, the nature of morality didn't change because we invented television. This then is a book about the future of the Enlightenment, and which argues that in spite of the emotion of this campaign, reason is still the best lamp against the darkness and difficulty of this world.

C.J.
London, May 2016

Postcript:

I would have liked to have ended this note there, but now, in late June of 2016, new developments need to be addressed. The swift movement of events to which I referred above rippled out eventually to affect even the title of this book. I began these pages as an Englishman living in an apparently outward-looking country which, proud of its history of tolerance and its democratic roots, and part of the European Union, seemed capable of looking across the Atlantic and observing the US elections from a position of confidence: nothing like the Trump phenomenon would ever be allowed to happen here. But by the time this book was about to go to press, that confidence had dramatically evaporated: to the dismay of this author, an unprecedentedly vile referendum campaign on Britain's membership in the European Union unfolded in the early summer of 2016. Again, facts ceased to matter; again, ignoble emotion triumphed over reason.

An awful pattern was emerging. One of the chief figures of the Leave campaign, the Justice Secretary Michael Gove, announced in the face of mounting evidence against his position from world leaders, the IMF, and the Bank of England (among many others) that he was 'tired of experts'. Then, in scenes grislier than any yet at a Trump rally, the kindly MP Jo Cox died outside her constituency surgery from multiple stab and gunshot wounds inflicted by a fanatic chanting the slogan 'Britain first!' Meanwhile the Leave.EU campaign released posters showing queues of supposedly frightening refugees – posters which seemed to imply, as Boris Johnson (the former Mayor of London and figurehead of the Leave campaign) was forced to admit, in distancing himself from them, that 'these were bad people'. By the 24th of June, the referendum had been won by Leave, and Prime Minister David Cameron, jubilantly elected a year beforehand, had resigned. To cap it all, Trump himself was on hand, on a visit to his golf course in Turnberry, to proclaim the unravelling of our political settlement 'a great thing'.

One is left to sigh at the occasional nimbleness of the devil. It all happened here with terrible suddenness: for hundreds of years one could say that the UK – like the US – was a tolerant place. Quite suddenly, one had to wonder whether that still held true. These recent events have at least served to crystallise matters. They show the fragility of democracy to be twofold: first, democracy is always threatened wherever there is violence. Whenever anyone stops arguing with their foe, and instead considers assaulting them (or worse), they are obviously not operating democratically. At Trump rallies, in the shocking shootings perpetrated by Omar Mateen in an Orlando nightclub on June 12th of 2016, and in the Cox murder, this worrying trend is now visible on both sides of the Atlantic. Second, democracy is under threat wherever a great deal of misinformation percolates. After the EU vote, Fox News reported that Britain had severed ties not with the EU, but with the UN. In the current climate, it might be too generous to call that a clerical slip – one wonders whether the newscasters know the difference between the two. On the day after the referendum, the most googled question was: 'What does it mean to leave the EU?' But the second most googled was 'What *is* the EU?' As we shall see throughout this book, this same kind of misinformation is rampant also in American politics. The democratic ideal is based on good faith as regards the sincere flow of information; where information is regularly falsified, the decision-making process goes awry unless a great deal of luck intervenes. Of course there will always be tension between the right to free speech, which might very well include making a controversial case, and the right of the people not to be bombarded with misinformation. The problem modern politics appears to face is that the former is enshrined in the laws of most democracies, while the latter, as things stand, is hardly protected at all. Will this change? In writing this book, I have often wished that it would.

In relation to all this, two literary parallels come to mind. The first is the couplet in Shakespeare's great Sonnet 65:

How with this rage shall beauty hold a plea,
Whose action is no stronger than a flower?

We have learned that democracy is delicate
like this; in its abstract way, it might even be
considered beautiful. The honest conversation
on which democracy is based is dependent on
mutual cooperation, and we see now how easily
that can be snapped: talking to one another can,
without much difficulty, become talking past
one another. The other text that springs to mind
is Euripides' play *Hippolytus*. In that work, the
eponymous hero is too proud to acknowledge the
power of Athena, Goddess of Love, but instead
elects to pursue the solitude of the hunt, and
the corresponding worship of the god Artemis.
Phaedra (to avoid complicating matters, we
shall not dwell on the fact that she is his step-
mother) dies for love of him. Hippolytus is exiled
by his father and rides out towards the destiny
of his banishment. Standing on a shore outside
the city walls, cut off from the possibilities of the
metropolis, this happens:

> Then, swelling still huger, and spattering
> from every side, it rushed seething
> and hissing to the shore, and straight

towards the chariot and the four horses. And in the very moment of bursting and crashing, the wave threw forth a monstrous savage bull, whose bellow filled the whole earth with an appalling echo, while the sight of him was too tremendous for mortal vision. The horses were seized with frenzy of terror.[0]

Hippolytus tries to calm the horses, but he has lost control of the reins. The isolation which he had assumed would protect him from problems proves more unwieldy than he had supposed. That bull, so strange and unexpected, coming out of nowhere with the terrifying logic of a predicament which might have been avoided, seems to me a satisfactory metaphor for today's extremism. It might be worthwhile in these times, when protectionism and anti-immigration policies have become so popular, to observe how Hippolytus got himself into such a pass: through bogus pride, withdrawal, and the abdication of the possibilities of interaction and love. Athena punishes him not for failing to love Phaedra (the play understands that that would be immoral) but for not loving at all.

This book may be read as a case study of this general trend; it might even be read with Euripides' great story in mind. Trump, Johnson, Gove – like Hippolytus, these men are not in control, one suspects, of the forces have unleashed. Trump, for instance, cut a panicky and curious figure at one rally before his airplane when there were whispers of a gunman in the crowd. He ducked desperately for cover: once the violence was turned on him, his fear was plain to see. Johnson likewise looked surprised by the ferocity with which he was booed outside his house on the morning after his victory in the EU referendum; a few days later he had to abandon his campaign when his apparent ally Michael Gove betrayed him and ran for the leadership himself. One notes that political friendships are hard to sustain when facts have not been agreed upon in the first place on which to base an agenda. In the end, we meet punishments and rewards which are essentially circular. Can there be any greater retribution for Donald Trump's deeds than to go on being Donald Trump in all his pettiness and greed and rage forever? Dante's *Inferno* is full of people serving that sentence: the universe metes out its justice precisely at the level of the self. But while all that is unfolding, those who stoke rage cause incalculable harm, and there are plenty doing so: we already see similar signs of the Hippolytus narrative in France, Poland, Germany, Hungary, and many others. Few would deny that it is a miserable spectacle.

But in these pages, the reader may also discover hope. It might be there in the very subject of this book. What we are herein examining is still, for all its faults, a vast democratic exercise – as indeed was the EU referendum. To disregard that fact would be to run the risk of alarmism: we are not yet discussing the end of American democracy, but we are discussing its frangibility. And as of 23rd June of 2016, we are not in the position just to call the American political process fragile. Our subject is now, by implication, the fragile nature of modern democracy itself, as it seems in this most troubled of years, 2016.

C.J.
4 July 2016

PROLOGUE – AN APRIL VISIT

If problems are transnational in nature, then they require a transnational response...
– President Barack Obama, 24th April, 2016.

Barack Obama visited the United Kingdom for the last time as President on the weekend of the 22nd April, 2016. He was ostensibly in London to celebrate the Queen's 90th birthday, but the dominant political issue was – and at time of writing, is – the referendum on Britain's continued membership of the European Union. It was known that Obama would intervene in the debate on the side of the Remain camp. In the event of it, his forthrightness came as a surprise – pleasant or otherwise, depending on your point of view. In a press conference alongside PM David Cameron, Obama was insistent about the remoteness of a hypothetical trade agreement between the United States and a post-Brexit United Kingdom, stating that a United Kingdom newly liberated from its ties with Europe would be 'at the back of the queue'[2] on trade. This appeared to injure the Brexit position: 'Leavers' had been hopeful of securing a quick bilateral agreement.

The remarks caused irritation in the Brexit camp. The United Kingdom Independence Party (UKIP) leader Nigel Farage, the spearhead of a single-issue party devoted to Britain's departure from the European Union, asked the electorate to disregard Obama's remarks, and apparently the views of all Americans: 'Who cares what they want?' The then London mayor Boris Johnson published an article in *The Sun* in which he attributed Obama's decision to move a bust of Winston Churchill out of the Oval Office to a 'part-Kenyan President's ancestral dislike of the British empire'.[3] The Brexit stalwart Dr. Liam Fox persuaded 100 Members of Parliament to sign a letter urging Obama not to intervene. Not everyone saw Obama's intervention in this way. Writing in *The Guardian*, Jonathan Freedland felt that the President had 'calmly ripped apart the case for Brexit'.[4] In short, people looked into his remarks and saw what they wanted. As Shakespeare has Maecenas say of Anthony in *Anthony and Cleopatra* 'When such a spacious mirror's set before him, he needs must see himself'.[5]

I raise this moment in US-UK relations advisedly. Obama defended in no uncertain terms his right to speak on UK politics: it was the case of the lion condescending to consider the plight of the mouse. In Britain today, when we look at the 2016 election campaign in the United States, the case is reversed: it is a case of the mouse looking warily up and, as in the Aesop fable, pleading for clemency.

Part of the interest of Obama's remarks is that the United Kingdom is now so rarely a point of worry for an American president. That Churchill bust might have caused controversy, but the British hegemony that Churchill fought to retain has long since been broken up. The Lend-Lease agreement of 1941 between Churchill and Roosevelt, though arrived at through the prism of friendship, was in its quiet way a power struggle which Churchill could never have been expected to win. Growing up today in the United Kingdom, one is conscious of something larger in the periphery of life. It is the planetary pull of – a word which can still send a shiver of thrill, or shudder of alarm – America.

In another sense, of course, the knowledge of America is also knowledge of one's own provinciality. The suspicion that real power is located elsewhere has many manifestations. There are those writers who, like Martin Amis or Christopher Hitchens, prefer Saul Bellow and

Philip Roth to any English novelist of the last seventy years. There is the British sports fan who stays up late to watch the Super Bowl; the movie fan who does the same for the Oscars. There are those who, from so much watching of US sitcoms, speak, without realising it, in a slight New York accent. And there are those who don't mind especially who the UK prime minister is at any one time, but mind very much the identity of the next US president. A friend once suggested that every citizen of the world should get a vote in the American presidential elections. The fact remains: from climate change to international terrorism, the condition of the Middle East, and the shape of the global economy, decisions are made in Rome and not Gaul. The 20th century was undoubtedly the American century. There is much talk of this one belonging to the Chinese. But America is still leagues ahead of any other country in the Global Presence Index, reflecting its combined economic, military and cultural clout. It isn't going away, and of course we don't really want it to go away. It's much too interesting.

THE AMERICAN POLITICAL PROCESS

Some of our fascination with American politics can be attributed to a pure love of theatre.

The United Kingdom seems not to be able to afford anything remotely approaching an American election. It might be that our billionaires prefer to spend their money on other things; we also, of course, have far fewer of them. But the American electoral process, if conducted in the UK, would look hilariously drawn-out and self-aggrandising. Campaigning for president is now a two-year job; running for prime minister, a mere six-week inconvenience, or about the amount of time a failed primary candidate in the US can expect to be on the road in Iowa. All presidents arrive in the Oval Office with both themselves and their staffs exhausted: they toil enormously even to get to the starting-line. The UK system can seem quaint by contrast. In the 2015-2016 primaries, on the Republican side, there were 12 debates and nine forums. More were demanded, but the front-runner Donald Trump refused. As the nominee, he will also need to conduct three further presidential debates, as well as numerous town halls, interviews and appearances. Our candidates are comparatively untested: in the 2015 UK general election, just the one debate was held. A UK election is also a comparatively inexpensive affair. In the 2010 general election, the Conservative party spent an embarrassingly meagre £16,682,874 – around double what the Labour Party raised, and three times the sum the Liberal Democrats raised.[6] Two years later, Obama would raise over one billion dollars for his re-election – more in fact than he was able to spend. Romney, the defeated candidate, raised just under that.[7] This version of democracy, awash with donations, was ratified by no less an authority than the US Supreme Court in the controversial case of *Citizens United v. Federal Election Committee*, in which the Court ruled that the First Amendment of the Constitution prohibited restrictions on donations of independent political expenditure, thus – rather ludicrously in the opinion of many – equating money with speech. 2016 is already a fantastically expensive election: *Bloomberg View* reports an overall projected cost of $10 billion, taking into account spending by candidates, political parties, and outside groups.[8]

Impressive though all this in one sense, one doesn't exactly sit through the American elections with unbroken admiration. It might be great theatre, but the play on view has always been crass, and never more so than this time around. America fell in love with Obama because he was able to bring wit and grace into an environment that appears designed to stymie it, whereas 2016 has been marked by the unprecedentedly ugly tone of the debate. Each day we turn on our TV screens to be reminded that there are few more unsightly things than political emotion. Dogmatic turns of mind are always unappealing – and yet elections are in part parades of narrow-mindedness and cliché. One does not win the nomination, one 'clinches' it, as if it were a thing in danger of being wrested from you right up until the last vote is counted – imagery that Al Gore would no doubt understand. One doesn't lose a nomination but 'suspends one's campaign', so that even in defeat the candidate at least gets to plant in the electorate's mind an intriguing sense of ellipsis. The debate itself is brought to us in dramatic cliché. One doesn't speak an opposing view, one 'fires back'; one doesn't have a simple disagreement but a 'row'; and one doesn't express a mild intention, one 'backs' things. Politics – that most pragmatic of arts – is increasingly enslaved to rhetoric: the hard-headedness and appreciation of legislative nuance required for the job forms no part of the interview process. The modern election has therefore become, at times, an exercise in pure noise. The process must also be predominantly dull for the candidates, all of whom are expected to repeat the same slogans, and parrot the same lines at a thousand political meetings. A candidate will only make news if he or she departs from the expected. This goes against the idea of the freewheeling and investigative mind – as epitomised by, for example, the much-loved Abraham Lincoln – which ought to delight in the surprising conclusion. A horrid discipline is at work: keeping to a bogus regime of parrying questions and – often – dedicated prevarication, is the best way to win the presidency.

All these trends have been at play for a long while. Obama both bucked them and left them in their place. He spoke with idealism, a sense of the historical moment, and even at times a poetry, which one doesn't normally associate with *Fox News*. But he wasn't about to risk losing the presidency by refusing a billion dollars in donations. Like so many politicians before him, he decided, having reasoned his own worth, that the most important thing was that he be elected, even if the system by which that process would happen could be shown to be faulty. Obama will leave in January 2017, yet the money will remain. And now, in Donald Trump, the 2016 election season has turned up a kind of emblem of all that is noisy, embarrassing and smug about money in America.

But it is possible also to look at an election like this one and feel that all human life is here: the yearning for a future that matches a sense of how life should be; interpretation of the past in order to author that future; the meaning of the nation state; the role of power in the world. Peace, love, hope, beauty – these large nouns, which seem so absent in any one-on-one with the candidates, are indeed at stake in an American election, absurd as that might seem. Indeed, they are hoisted before our very eyes in the modern context, not as abstractions but in relation to the difficulty of their realisation – as the only things worth braving the mess of politics for. The power of America ramps up the stakes for all of us, with each election more critical than the last, like some terrible gambling habit.

UPON THE HEALTH OF DEMOCRACY

All this has terrific consequences. America isn't just an example of modern democracy – it *is* modern democracy. Our system – and its European counterparts – may be heading the American way: more noise, more focus on personalities over issues, more money.

We are watching an ancient process active in the modern world. Over 2,000 years ago, the way people looked at their affairs in a small city in Greece underwent a revolution. The story is known in broad terms, but watching the Trump phenomenon unfold, one suspects there is no harm in repeating it: by around 508 BC, as a result of the influence of Cleisthenes, all nobles – the early Athenians weren't so open-minded about the poor – were permitted to attend the *ecclesia*, or assembly. The idea was devastatingly simple: decisions shouldn't be hidden away, but undertaken openly. The thing to avoid was the tyrant, the strong man – the pre-TV Donald Trump. In time, Pericles would arrive at this fuller definition of democracy – or rather Thucydides would arrive at it through the mouth of Pericles:

Its administration favors the many instead of the few; this is why it is called a *democracy*. If we look to the laws, they afford equal justice to all in their private differences; if to social standing, advancement in public life falls to reputation for capacity, class considerations not being allowed to interfere with merit; nor again does poverty bar the way, if a man is able to serve the state, he is not hindered by the obscurity of his condition.[9]

2016, like all election years, is a staging-post on the journey of that idea. Democracy proved difficult from time to time. The Roman Republic ceded to the Caesars: a notable setback. Nero, in retrospect, was about as ill-suited to power, and just as strangely inseparable from it, as is Donald Trump. The idea of democracy went underground. It would prove resilient enough to keep resurfacing, but fragile enough to be continually threatened. The Divine Right of Kings eventually gave way to the Enlightenment, with its connotations of an experiential basis for government. Most of us think of democracy as something granite-tough – or to use Whitman's phrase, the force which can 'make inseparable cities with their arms about each other's necks'. But there have been few instances of its arising in history, when it hasn't eventually been challenged by some brutal clique or by a Strong Man. In the 20th century, Nazism and Stalinism – as well as a rich menu of autocracies, oligarchies, military dictatorships and Islamic theocracies – all grew up in direct opposition to liberal democracy. Chaos is stubborn.

The Obama Brexit moment might therefore be seen as a chance to pose another question: 'Are vast nation states even suited to Athenian-style democracy?' Obama would say that yes, they can be. The President has got to where he is by inclining towards optimism on that score: he will never admit that something is broken without in the next breath announcing that he is on the cusp of fixing it. But voters still rail against a distant technocracy. Certain cities – Washington, Brussels – have become names to spit out contemptuously.

Is America vulnerable to the Nero chaos? There are worrying signs – we shall look in detail at Donald Trump in Chapter Five – but there are also consoling indicators, both with respect to what the outgoing Obama administration has achieved, and in the general direction of America towards a more tolerant society. But perhaps the real sign of ill-health is the election itself. In its original Grecian incarnation, the emphasis of democracy was always on debate. Now it is on the process of getting elected. Once a symposium, democracy has become, under the American model, a search. What are we searching for? The wish is for the great man – what Kiekergaard calls in *The Book of Adler*, the extraordinarius. In electing Obama, Americans elected someone they suspected of being such a man. Trump – and to a certain extent, Ted Cruz and Bernie Sanders – have at various times, and for different people, appeared to fulfil this same need in 2016. Meanwhile Hillary Clinton, by not claiming to be anything more than a knowledgeable pro, has been hurt repeatedly at the polls. The modern candidate can no longer risk running as anything other than the answer to all problems.

In his 1754 cycle of paintings *Humours of an Election* (Figure 1), William Hogarth showed how easily the noble idea of democracy can degenerate into the silliness of elections: here in these teeming canvases, we find the same vile caricatures of foreigners (in Hogarth's satire

Jews, in this election the Muslim population),
the same intimidation that 2016 has already seen
at Trump rallies (Figure 2), and the jingoism
we see all the time in the question that always
permeates a general election in the US: not just
'What is America?' but 'What is American?'

What indeed? One might say it is
a question so important that citizens feel
compelled to pose it every four years.

Fig. 1. W. Hogarth, *Chairing the Member*, *The Humours of an Election
series*, (1755).[10] Painted over 250 years ago, this image shows how, in
their essence, elections don't change. It is not perhaps so different
from the tumult at a Trump rally in Fig. 2 below.[11]

'OBAMA OUT'

So said President Obama, dropping the mic at
the end of his last White House Correspondents
Dinner. It might be seen as a kind of starting-
gun: all elections are referenda on what has
gone before.

But it must be said that in 2008, Obama
came up with an exceptionally compelling set
of answers to the question: 'What is America?'
He said, in effect: 'America is me, in all the
heterogeneity of my makeup, in my can-do
approach, in my reasonableness, and in my
intelligence.' He said repeatedly 'Yes, we can'.
He might well have meant the 'we' part, but

it often sounded like 'I'. But then he was the extraordinarius.

It didn't work out exactly as his supporters wished. One has an image of all those 2008 posters of Hope and Change gathering dust and mould in attics these past eight years. The fact that the election of an extraordinarius didn't solve every American problem, let alone every global one, has created a range of reactions, and we see these playing out in the 2016 election. On the one hand, there are those who would elect another extraordinarius, only of a different kind. The followers of Trump and of Bernie Sanders (see Chapter Eight) spring to mind here. There are those who are happy with the broad direction and achievements of the Obama administration, and are therefore content to accept a kind of caretaker administration in the shape of the technocrat Hillary Clinton (see Chapter Seven). More generally, it has been possible for certain intellectuals to pose as weary of the political class as a whole, including Obama. The Nobel-winning economist Joseph Stiglitz for instance, often sounds in his book *The Great Divide* as irritated with Obama as with George W. Bush. This attitude, weary with politics in all its mess and inevitable disappointment, will no doubt make some stay away from the polls, as some always do. It can seem as if nothing serious-minded or substantial was attempted in the Obama administration.

This election isn't just about the health of democracy – that is in some sense always the case every time an election is staged. It is really about the health of the enlightenment, even its ongoing viability. The two ideas – democracy and enlightenment – of course, go hand in hand: democracy in Athens coincides with the tremendous flowering of philosophy and literature that gave us Socrates, Plato, Aristotle, Sophocles, Aeschylus, Euripides and all the rest. It is an essentially intelligent idea. Where it is in health, one expects to find great achievement going on under its protective wing. When it is in decline, we are all the poorer.

The Obama Brexit intervention, though fleeting and minor, was a moment of dialogue in a wider conversation undertaken in a shared language: the language of international cooperation. In his famous funeral oration which I quoted above, Pericles also states: 'we are rather a pattern to others than imitators ourselves'. He could hardly have said anything more prophetic. One of the great questions of our times is what the nation state means in a global world. But there is, one suspects, a still greater matter. How do we solve transnational problems? The answer is that we need to agree on a set of principles with which to tackle them. We need to use the Enlightenment.

But that will be very difficult if a major party in the world's most powerful nation has little regard for it, as we shall see in the next chapters.

PART 1

THE 2016 ELECTION AND THE ENLIGHTENMENT

CHAPTER ONE – THE ENLIGHTENMENT V. CHAOS

I'm, like, a really smart person.
– Donald Trump, 2015

Where to start in telling the story of this election? You might begin with Obama's 2008 win, the crowds thundering with 'Yes, we can' and jostling with Change signs. The story might then be about thwarted hope – or, if you prefer, the way in which fulfilled promise looks so much less appealing than promise itself. You might go further back and consider Hillary Clinton as First Lady of the United States and scrutinise her features when she first hears about a woman named Monica Lewinsky: that might segue into a tale of stoical redemption, if you wish. More dramatically, you could travel back to Donald Trump's wedding to Melania Knauss on January 22nd 2005 in Palm Beach, Florida: among the guests, then Senator for New York Hillary Clinton and her husband Bill. An enterprising photographer catches the Clintons and the new Trumps laughing together, not knowing what lies ahead of them. Or perhaps you would prefer some quiet scene in Trump Tower: Donald Trump, looking in the mirror perhaps, the pinched and ruminative mouth – like the knot in a balloon – mulling over the state of the Republican Party: there's an opportunity there for the right man at the right time, he thinks.

I prefer to begin further back – in 1939, in the opening days of World War II, when W.H. Auden, a newly-arrived émigré, sat in his famous dive on Fifty-Second Street and in his poem 'September 1, 1939' imagined his immediate future as one in which the enlightenment was driven away, and the world would suffer 'mismanagement' and 'grief'.[12]

'The enlightenment driven away'. Auden was, of course, trying to guess what war with Nazism would bring. But today his lines rush out from the time he wrote them – as a poet's words are meant to do – to describe a time he couldn't have guessed at. They make one think of the US in 2016. They are a reminder that political rage is a contagion which can strike anywhere. They are an echo of fear. Obliquely, they are a comment on this election.

AN UNPRECEDENTED ELECTION

In a system of perpetual elections, someone is
always electioneering. No sooner had the dust
settled on Obama's second general election
victory against Mitt Romney than the field began
to form. Hillary Clinton had already left the State
Department to take a rest in order to prepare
for her run. In Vermont, a little-known senator,
Bernie Sanders, was pondering his. Gripped
by rage, Senator Ted Cruz of Texas began to
crusade for a defunding of Obamacare: he too
would enter the race. Donald Trump, who had
flirted with a run in 2012, sat in Trump Tower and
pondered a contract for the next season of *The
Apprentice*. The pen hovered, and the signature
was withheld. Perhaps he thought a stab at the
presidency might be more fun. Jeb Bush and
Marco Rubio in Florida were beginning to lock
up money from the Republican establishment.
John Kasich in Ohio had in his small way done
the same. Gore Vidal once wrote: 'Apparently, a
democracy is a place where numerous elections
are held at great cost without issues and with
interchangeable candidates'.[13] Here again,
then, were the candidates, prepared to endure
the media round – to oblige in the hunt for

soundbites, risk being on the receiving end of a 'gotcha' moment, to jump through the election hoops, and try and emerge on the other end hearing 'Hail to the Chief' on a cold January day.

And yet something else had snuck on stage. Rage, a sense of disenfranchised resentment, was in the hearts of millions of Americans. This anger, its force and extent – and the presence of candidates prepared to pool it for their own ends, not to mention a media establishment prepared to push the story – is what gives this election its unique, and uniquely alarming, character. Rage is always asking to be listened to – it is never asking for enlightenment, but courting chaos.

THE RAGE AGAINST THE MACHINE

How did the possibility of chaos even arise in the first place? Put simply, it has its origins – at least in part – in disappointment. The promise of the Obama administration hadn't yielded a complete fix. Unemployment might have halved since 2009, but as the first candidates began to declare, the apparent good news wasn't uppermost in people's minds: the majority of

Americans have experienced stagnant wages since the Great Recession of 2008. At the same time, America's standing in the world, though it has begun to recover since the miserable days of Abu Ghraib under President Bush, remains shaky. Substantial reduction of military presence in Iraq and Afghanistan has created anxiety among those who once found repose in the thought that they lived in an endlessly powerful country. A large number of white blue-collar workers had begun to wonder if it might all be the fault of Muslims and Hispanics, people outside their ken. Voters were also feeling increasingly angry at 'Washington'. During the Obama years, behaviour there had been more than usually counter-productive and childish, particularly in Congress. Washington had become a name to spit out in contempt, as if it were not just a place of marked legislative dysfunction, but a city of Stygian gloom where the damned reside.

Aristotle wrote that man learns by imitation; we regress similarly. Over the next period, up until 2016, a contagion of anger would affect all sides of the political spectrum, and alter the tone of political discourse. On the Democrat side, the election would showcase an increasingly bitter feud between Hillary Clinton and Bernie Sanders, culminating in an especially raucous showdown in New York. More worryingly, anger on the right would lead to miserable developments. A Black Lives Matter activist, Mercutio Southall Jr., was beaten up at one of Donald Trump's rallies in November of 2015. This violence was endorsed by the candidate: 'Maybe he should have been roughed up'. It was a sign of things to come. In his announcement – looked at in detail in Chapter Five – Trump ascribed the country's ills to immigration. By December 7th, 2015, in the wake of the Paris terror attacks, Trump had released the following memorandum:

> Donald J. Trump is calling for a total and complete shutdown of Muslims entering the United States until our country's representatives can figure out what is going on.[14]

Like this, the rage grew as emotive language fell into place: 'total and complete' sounds like someone ranting in the corner of a bar. The angry tone and the cruel nature of Trump's proposals have contributed to an air of unreality. On a policy level, it was difficult then, as now, to imagine the criteria for readmission were such a shutdown ever to take place. The policies were called unworkable, and indeed it was very difficult to see how they would ever be administered in the first place. But history is to some extent the story of successful discrimination against minorities. And, as we shall see, Trump – more than any other Republican candidate – had tapped a mood.

Throughout the end of 2015 and at the start of 2016, Trump's approval rating soared in a crowded field of 17 candidates. In late January, Trump freewheeled again to violent imagery: 'I could stand in the middle of Fifth Avenue and shoot somebody and not lose any votes'. At least with regard to the Republican electorate, he had spoken a kind of truth. By February 9th, Trump had won more than double the votes of any other candidate in the New Hampshire primary. By May 4th, following his victory in Indiana – and in spite of numerous attempts to stop him – he became the presumptive nominee.

But Trump was not necessarily the most radical figure that the Republican Party had put forward. As we shall see in Chapter Six, for many Republicans and Democrats, Ted Cruz – government-slashing and fiercely ideological – was the more dangerous candidate.

It was a measure of Republican panic – and the radicalism of Trump – that the establishment in the last months of the race adopted Cruz as their candidate. Added to this have been concerning trends across the Republican Party. To doubt climate change, to oppose same-sex marriage, to favour mass deportations of 'illegal immigrants', to rail against Obamacare – all these things have become orthodoxy on the American right.

What happens if one party becomes divorced from reality or even becomes fundamentally unkind? Will a Democrat be returned to the White House on and on until the Republican Party rights itself?

Or will the pendulum swing toward chaos, because in a two-party system, dissatisfied with Democratic rule, it has nowhere else to swing?

A BRIEF HISTORY OF RAGE IN AMERICA

History would – at least on the face of it – caution against too much pessimism.

America has functioned, with varying success, as a democracy for more than two centuries. At the presidential level alone, it has thrown up some of the great figures in world history –Thomas Jefferson, Abraham Lincoln, Franklin D. Roosevelt, arguably Obama himself. America's voters have a reasonable track record of good sense. Though there have been inconsequential and incompetent presidents – even crooked ones like Richard Nixon – there has never been anything to compare to the possibility of a President Trump.

But beneath the surface it has always teemed with tensions: it is a country conceived in revolution, delivered in civil war, and has had numerous growing pains since. Strife has flared repeatedly. Like all countries, it has cruelty in its past – of a sort that a particular kind of politician might exploit. It is a place of sudden spasms: from the miserable treatment of Chinese immigrants in the late 1800s or the Know Nothing anti-Catholic movement of the 1850s to Jim Crow and The Civil War itself, there has always been a strain in American life which, like Donald Trump, has been happy to emphasise and not mend racial differences, and has been content with alarmism.

There has also – as in 2016 – long been rage about the size of government, and Auden would have known about that when

he sat down to write his poem: in the modern
era, it starts with Franklin Delano Roosevelt.
In the wake of the 1929 Wall Street Crash,
and the subsequent Great Depression, FDR
implemented his New Deal – a series of
government programs designed to relieve the
poor and regulate the financial system. FDR's
1936 landslide against Alf Landon had certain
similarities to the 2016 race. In a speech at
Madison Square Gardens three days before
the election, Roosevelt had railed against: 'the
old enemies of peace: business and financial
monopoly, speculation, reckless banking, class
antagonism, sectionalism, war profiteering.' He
added cheerfully: 'They are unanimous in their
hate for me – and I welcome their hatred.'[15] It is
possible to detect echoes of the present time.
A Democratic President with considerable
political skills becomes unbeatable in general
elections. He embarks on an expansion of the
federal government. It earns him a new coalition,
but also enrages those – the financiers, and the
businessmen who have a stake in the status
quo. The 2016 election provides this difference:
this time, America has found a billionaire who
poses as the champion of the working-class and
whom his fellow billionaires are plainly alarmed

by. Trump is – from their perspective – the wrong billionaire.

The two threads – rage about perceived economic injustice, and resistance to immigration – combined in the 1930s in a still darker way. In his 2004 novel *The Plot Against America*, Philip Roth would imagine an alternative history of the period in which its darkest forces had been unleashed. The opening lines of the novel set the tone: 'Fear presides over these memories, a perpetual fear'.[16] Roth puts real figures and events into his fiction: Nazi-sympathising aviator Charles Lindbergh wins the Republican nomination for president and embarks on a round of repressive measures against Jews. The book asks us to consider the possibility that America was not so far away from embracing then the solutions that it is considering again now.

Roth was able to bring in much more than just Lindbergh. 1938 had also seen Father Charles Coughlin reprint in weekly instalments the anti-Semitic *The Protocols of the Elders of Zion*, a text beloved by Hamas today, which envisages a Jewish conspiracy to seize the world. These views were not so different from Henry Ford's, who Roth also includes in his novel, and whose newspaper *The Dearborn Independent*, in addition to reprinting *The Protocols*, was forced to close after printing numerous anti-Semitic articles. The question of whether Donald Trump is a fascist will be looked at in Chapter Five, but for now it must simply be said that today's radicalism in America has its precursors. The notion of a President Trump may seem ridiculous, but broadly Trumpist elements have long lurked in the American organism, and have even seemed to prosper from time to time.

THE ENLIGHTENMENT – BIG 'E', LITTLE 'E'

Of course America's enlightened aspects have so far tended to win through. When Auden wrote of 'the enlightenment driven away', what precisely was he worried about losing?

The 2016 election returns time and again to the question of what America means, and so it is worth remembering that it was created along avowedly Enlightenment ideals. It is true that two of the Enlightenment's most prominent early figures, John Locke and Thomas Hobbes, disagree on the nature of government. Locke believed that the Divine Right of Kings derived from the *consent* of the governed. Thomas Hobbes, meanwhile, believed that humankind was caught up in such a miserable predicament that people in their natural state would submit to the state to escape fear – their only shot was to surrender their rights to it. In America, Locke won – at least on the face of the deed. Thomas Jefferson's The Declaration of Independence is an essentially Lockeian document:

> We hold these truths to be self-evident, that all men are created equal, that they are endowed by their Creator with certain unalienable Rights, that among these are Life, Liberty and the pursuit of Happiness. –That to secure these rights, Governments are instituted among Men, deriving their just powers from *the consent of the governed*, –That whenever any Form of Government becomes destructive of these ends, it is the Right of the People to alter or to abolish it, and to institute new Government, laying its foundation on such principles and organizing its powers in such form, as to them shall seem most likely to effect their Safety and Happiness. [italics mine]

America then is built on rights – and the expectation that the people will insist on them. Government is presented as something pliable, an ongoing project the governed are always refining to assist in the creation of a better life for themselves: the state *is* the wishes of the governed. This sounds, because it is, eminently sensible. One cannot help but note in passing the reference to Safety and Happiness: it is impossible to imagine Jefferson looking on at, for example, the 2012 Sandy Hook massacre, when Adam Lanza killed 20 children at an elementary school, without thinking that some revision to the nation's gun laws might add to the 'Safety and Happiness' of the nation.

Enlightenment values can be found further back than Locke and Jefferson. The idea of a 'self-evident truth', for instance, derives from the Enlightenment idea of experiment. This was best articulated by the English philosopher Francis Bacon in his *Novum Organum*. The second half of the following quote strikes me as a sensible place to begin when it comes to the business of problem-solving in government, and I have placed it in italics:

There remains simple experience; which, if taken as it comes, is called accident; if sought for, experiment. But this kind of experience is no better than a broom without its band, as the saying is – a mere groping, as of men in the dark, that feel all around them for the chance of finding their way, when they had much better way for daylight, or light a candle, and then go. *But the true method of experience, on the contrary, first lights the candle, and then by means of the candle shows the way; commencing as it does with experience duly ordered and digested, not bungling or erratic, and from it deducing axioms, and from established axioms again new experiments...*[17]

This approach to problems has great pedigree. When we strap ourselves into a plane and calmly order a glass of wine, we are trusting this method. When we aren't feeling well and book an appointment at the doctor's, we are also trusting it. Yet the 2016 elections show, as we shall see, that a significant portion of the Republican Party appears to distrust it. By contrast, Baconian experiment has been the stated method of the Obama administration. The data-driven approach to government didn't start with Obama, but his administration was from the outset openly cerebral. President Obama is fond of quoting the line from the 2015 film *The Martian*: 'Let's science the heck out of this'. At a time when the issue of global warming is agreed to be an urgent one, Republican hostility to the scientific approach may yet have dire implications for not only the health of America, but also for the welfare of the planet.

Can we then go further? The Enlightenment refers to the advances of a particular group of philosophers at a particular time, but Auden refers to enlightenment – with a small 'e'. This takes us further back. It can mean something as apparently simple as behaving intelligently. I find an excellent example of what this might mean in Charles Nicholl's descriptions of the notebooks of Leonardo da Vinci:

> The great lesson of the manuscripts is that everything is to be questioned, investigated, peered into, worried away at, brought back to first principles.[18]

This small 'e' enlightenment of course encompasses the whole history of human cleverness. Its origins are rich and deep, and it is, one would hope, absurd to imagine us parted from it as the result of these elections. But the global and interconnected nature of our world is a warning against hubris on this score. We shall touch on climate change frequently in this book, but there are also economic challenges and serious foreign policy matters which the next president will face, and which will require an exceptionally cool head. Besides, in the fall of the Roman Empire, and in the fascist regimes of the 20th century, history also serves up several unpleasant examples of societies that had assumed that their way of life would continue, but which were forced to confront their fallibility.

In 2016, one is repeatedly reminded that these general considerations and forebodings – the wish for enlightenment and the fear of chaos – come into being or fail to come into being according to the human material that comes along at any given time.

So what has been the tendency of American life these last years?

CHAPTER 2 – THE ENLIGHTEN-MENT FROM FDR TO OBAMA

He's unusually incurious, abnormally unintelligent, amazingly inarticulate, fantastically uncultured, extraordinarily uneducated and apparently quite proud of all of these things.[19]

– Christopher Hitchens, on President George W. Bush

Agree or disagree with the following statement:
It is broadly true to say that America proceeded on a reasonably enlightened course from 1945 – not just the year of WWII's end, but also the year of the death of FDR – via Kennedy and Reagan, until President Barack Obama's election in 2008.

In deciding one way or the other, we run up against the paradox of history. On the one hand, the years in question gave the world an America broadly inclined to do good. During that time, American culture was exported around the world. America made you tap your foot or sing along to Elvis Presley, Bob Dylan, Simon and Garfunkel, Nirvana, and Beyoncé. *The Simpsons, Seinfeld,* and *Curb Your Enthusiasm* proved that America could make you laugh. *The West Wing, The Wire,* and *The Good Wife* showed that America could make you waste your evening and yet know that it had not been wasted. Frank Capra told you about a cheerful America; Martin Scorsese showed you it was really noir. The novels of Philip Roth were funny and outrageous; Saul Bellow's books teemed with intellectuals and street vendors; John Updike's tales were like fine lace; Toni Morrison's engendered sympathetic rage.

In poetry, if you liked rhyme, you had Robert Frost — but if you didn't, it didn't matter, there were Berryman, Ginsberg, Armantrout, and a thousand more. During that same period, Neil Armstrong walked on the moon; Einstein moved to Princeton; Bill Gates founded Microsoft then let you know, by setting up the Bill & Melinda Gates Foundation, that money wasn't all that mattered to him. Communism fell as the Soviet Union seemed to concede the superiority of the American way of life. Relations opened with China. Even President George W. Bush, few people's favourite commander-in-chief, pledged $5 billion a year to fight AIDS in Africa. It was an American who cured your polio, or gave you that Hepatitis B vaccine. An American designed your iPhone, and then your updated iPhone. The results were in: America could make you happy. It did this while remaining a democracy. It did this *because* it was a democracy.

Yet on a parallel track, a less attractive America struggled to be born. Wars in Korea, Vietnam, and Iraq caused enormous loss of life for little discernible benefit. There was a sense that when the US *was* needed, it did nothing – as in Rwanda. During the 1980s, inequality rose dramatically. The rich began to seem braggarty, perhaps deliberately pig-headed. There remained a troublesome gap between the benign way in which America viewed itself and the damage it was capable of doing, or of turning a blind eye to. *American History X*, *American Sniper*, *American Beauty* – all enjoyable films, but the country plainly has a self-mythologizing tendency. Perhaps this made it blind to its faults. But if you were inclined to wonder at the possible solipsism of Hollywood, then you would probably have to admit that it was the least of America's problems. The briefest glance at incarceration figures was enough to tell you that the civil rights movement was incomplete. When Bob Dylan said that every song he wrote was really about the Civil War, he was pointing out that its wounds hadn't healed. For many, the famous dream of Dr. Martin Luther King Jr. had ceded to a nightmare of discrimination and all its inherent frustrations.

Anyone who wished to take this second view of the country could point to a cast of villains – whether it be Senator Joe McCarthy (with his witch-hunt against Communists), Richard Nixon, or, later on, Dick Cheney.

2016 can sometimes feel like a fight between these two countries: one which is open, comfortable with diversity, and tolerant. And the other – suspicious of complexity, harsh, even cruel.

THE INTELLIGENCE QUESTION

Richard Nixon, who served from 1969 until his resignation in 1974 as the country's 37th president, provides an important watershed in an issue that has come to matter increasingly in modern American politics and which is especially important in 2016 – namely, the intelligence (or lack thereof) of the candidates. Nixon's fatal flaw was not the absence of intellect many would later note in, say, George W. Bush or Sarah Palin, but too much of it. Here is Clive James reviewing Nixon's memoir:

> Unfortunately for himself, America and the world, Nixon could never see his

strength for what it was. He was forever
augmenting it with unnecessary cunning.
If he had been less clever he might have
lasted longer. But he always felt that he
needed an edge – he had to get the bulge
on the other guy.[20]

In this instance, 'getting the bulge on the other
guy', and being too clever, meant impeachment
proceedings. It could be argued that the
trauma of Nixon's resignation still lurks in
the Republican Party today. Post-Watergate,
the electorate looked for other qualities than
intellect in their Presidents. Particularly
among Republicans, intelligence had become
associated with a certain Machiavellianism.

The uninspiring integrity of Jimmy
Carter followed – Carter was almost as much
an outsider to his party's nomination as was
Trump, or as Sanders would have been. He
lost the Presidency to the sunny optimist
and ex-actor Ronald Reagan. Martin Amis
described Reagan in a piece in 1979 which feels
prophetic today: 'His style is one of hammy self-
effacement, a wry dismay at his own limited
talents and their drastic elevation'.[21] Amis'
friend Christopher Hitchens would later write a

piece for *Slate* entitled 'The Stupidity of Ronald Reagan'. Reagan remains revered on the right –Trump and his supporters often attempt to compare him to Reagan, but Amis' description is now instantly recognisable: it is the cry of literary alarm about a Republican candidate's basic intelligence.

In the event of it, the Great Communicator, as Reagan was known, would prove so popular that his style has never really gone away: never again those Nixonian smarts; instead, you must 'tell it like it is'. George W. Bush was a kind of eight-year long impersonation of Reagan. Sarah Palin, John McCain's disastrous pick for vice-president when he was the Republican nominee in the race against Barack Obama in 2008, might be seen as a dangerous mutation of the Reagan gene.

But Reagan had been underestimated by the liberal intelligentsia. Not all that he did looks as good now as it might have done before the Great Recession of 2008-2009: the inequality which is such a potent issue in 2016 was essentially his doing. But no one now prefers Brezhnev's dreary memoirs to Reagan's entertaining diaries, and the Soviet Union did collapse on his watch. He set a template of

folksy homespunness. Reagan's legacy – partly
because it is easy to be a transformational
president when you plan to cut things, and also
because of luck – seems secure as that of a
substantial president. But to an unusual degree,
this success has meant emulation – and also
to an unusual degree that emulation has been
disastrous.

THE FIRST CLINTON

After the relatively uncompelling George H.W.
Bush presidency came the election of Bill
Clinton. For liberals, it promised more than it
delivered.

Clinton's announcement in his 1996
State of the Union address that the era of
big government was over represented the
ratification of Reaganism by an apparently
superior mind. A Rhodes Scholar with a law
degree from Yale, Clinton has an intelligence
about which anecdotes continue to trickle in to
this day.[22] Clinton espoused a Third Way, in which
his government would address social injustice
while also leaving the market bequeathed to him
by Reagan and George H.W. Bush unregulated.
Critics still argue that he was more successful

in protecting the free market than in addressing social problems.

After eight years of Obama – and especially with the 2016 Bernie Sanders campaign in mind – some of Clinton's policies now look strange coming from a Democratic president. Clinton returned to Arkansas in the middle of his first presidential campaign to affirm the execution of Ricky Ray Rector, an intellectually impaired inmate on death row who said he was saving his last meal, pecan pie, for after his execution. Clinton also instituted the much-loathed 'Don't Ask, Don't Tell' policy – subsequently repealed by Obama – which barred gays and bisexuals from openly serving in the military. Another betrayal for liberals was the effective repeal of the Glass-Steagall Act, which freed up the activity of banks, a move which is today considered a major contributing factor to the 2008-2009 Great Recession. This side of Bill Clinton's record – supported by Hillary Clinton – should be borne in mind when we come to discuss her in Chapter Seven.

Today what is interesting is that Clinton's acceptance of Reaganism did not prevent the creation of a new partisanship in Washington. Clinton's intelligence won him elections, but his accommodations with free-market economics won him no fans in the Republican Party, and plenty of critics among Democrats. Instead of cooperation between parties, a certain childishness entered the national discourse in the Clinton years. It continues to this day. This immaturity was exemplified by the Starr Report. Originally commissioned to look into the Clintons' real estate investments in the Whitewater Development Corporation, and into the suicide of Deputy White House Counsel Vince Foster, Starr soon expanded his investigations into the President's sexual liaisons. Vindictiveness had been permitted free rein – Republicans began to show that, if forced to sit out governing the executive branch, then they would not necessarily be equable about it. Even the initial investigation into Foster's death wasn't carried out with the appropriate regret but instead with a partisan glee. Clinton was carrying his anger with him years later:

> I heard a lot of the right-wing talk show people...and all the sleazy stuff they said. They didn't give a rip that he had killed himself or that his family was miserable or that they could break the hearts [of

Foster's friends and family]. It was
just another weapon to slug us with, to
dehumanize us with.[23]

The 2000 race – a face-off between Clinton's
Vice-President Al Gore and George W. Bush
– therefore took place in an atmosphere of
mutual distrust. The outcome of that election
seems almost to have been designed to stoke
those divisions. In 2016, we are still living in its
aftermath. The election of George W. Bush will
always be controversial because, as everyone
knows, it isn't clear that he was elected at all.
The votomatic punch-card system used in
Florida – on whose 29 Electoral College votes
the contest hinged – didn't work, and we will
never know what result a state-wide recount
would have given. The Supreme Court heard the
case of *Bush v. Gore*, and a judgement authored
by Justice Scalia, a vocal Republican who
could hardly have been expected to wish for the
opposing result and whom we shall be hearing
more of in Chapter Nine, awarded the presidency
to Bush. To the petty grievance of the Clinton
years was added this blurry result and all the
conflicting emotions that naturally arose from it.

Yet in 2000, the present situation of rancour hadn't quite been reached.

On the one hand, Bush, for all his bluntness, did have a kind of Reaganish charm, which independents were not wholly immune to. Even before the 2001 September 11th attacks on the World Trade Center, Bush's approval ratings regularly topped 60% – unimaginable territory for Obama today.

In addition, the Democrats, having experienced the obstructionist tactics of the Republican leadership, both in the Starr Report and under the outlandish speakership of Newt Gingrich, decided against those same tactics. There are no instances in the Bush administration, during the years when Nancy Pelosi was Speaker of the House, of Democrats refusing to raise the debt ceiling and fund the government, as John Boehner would later do under President Obama. But the main reason for the atmosphere of relative civility was that the 9/11 attacks on the World Trade Center, perpetrated by Al-Qaeda, brought the country together, temporarily at least, under Bush's leadership.

Many Democrats, including future Secretaries of State Hillary Clinton and John

Kerry, voted with the Bush administration to authorise the subsequent invasion of Iraq in 2003. It is true that these accommodations existed alongside ongoing mutterings within the Democratic Party about the lost election. But the impression is that the Democrats behaved more forgivingly under Bush than Republicans had done under Clinton, or would do under Obama. Later on, Pelosi would refuse to back the calls by some Democrats that Bush be impeached on account of providing false information leading up to the invasion of Iraq.

THE 'STUPID' PRESIDENT

And yet that doesn't mean things were entirely civil, because there was one other factor that entered national life during the Bush administration. It was the allegation that the 43rd President of the United States was stupid.

I began this chapter with Christopher Hitchens' famous denunciation of Bush's intellectual powers. This was no one-off. During the Bush years, the idea that Bush wasn't intelligent was more than a regularly heard gripe: it was almost an industry. Books of 'Bushisms' detailed the President's amusing verbal blunders: 'Rarely is the question asked, is our children learning.' And everyone knows the rather charming slip: 'They misunderestimated me.' On top of this literature, there were numerous *YouTube* videos of Bush bloopers. Footage of Bush trying to leave a press conference in China and failing to open a door was gleefully replayed. David Letterman ran a Top 10 of favourite George Bush moments. Bush took it in good part and didn't seem particularly to mind: an optimistic anti-intellectualism had been a hallmark of his campaign. Bush's use of the phrase 'fuzzy math' during the 2000 presidential debates to describe Al Gore's economic arguments had apparently helped, not hindered him. Even so, the refrain became that not only had the election been stolen, but it had been stolen *by a stupid person from an intelligent person*.

This narrative of a stupid President may not have stung Bush himself but it was battled by some Republicans, and is sometimes still battled. In 2013, Keith Hennessey, former Assistant to the US President for Economic Policy and Director of the US National Economic Council, wrote a piece called 'George W. Bush is smarter than you', in which he quotes himself as addressing a class at Stanford Business School:

Don't take it personally, but President Bush is smarter than almost every one of you. Were he a student here today, he would consistently get "HP" (High Pass) grades without having to work hard, and he'd get an "H" (High, the top grade) in any class where he wanted to put in the effort.

Hennessey goes on to assure the class of Bush's gifts. He wasn't the first to do so. Even during the Bush administration itself, Karl Rove, a senior advisor to George W. Bush, had let it be known that he was in a 'reading contest' with the President. This article, one of the stranger I have seen in *The Wall Street Journal*, can sometimes seem to protest too much. In this passage, Rove impresses us with the President's reading list:

> The nonfiction ran from biographies of Abraham Lincoln, Andrew Carnegie, Mark Twain, Babe Ruth, King Leopold, William Jennings Bryan, Huey Long, LBJ and Genghis Khan to Andrew Roberts's "A History of the English Speaking Peoples Since 1900," James L. Swanson's "Manhunt," and Nathaniel Philbrick's "Mayflower." Besides eight Travis McGee

novels by John D. MacDonald, Mr. Bush tackled Michael Crichton's "Next," Vince Flynn's "Executive Power," Stephen Hunter's "Point of Impact," and Albert Camus's "The Stranger," among others... To my surprise, the president demanded a rematch in 2007.[24]

It is impossible to discover the truth of this claim – except to say that people who really read tend not to do so competitively but with casual pleasure. Rove states that he won the first 'read-off' in 2006 by 110-95 (presumably meant to seem a noble defeat for a busier and more stressed-out President), and the 2007 contest by 51 to 76. Another Pyrrhic victory for the President no doubt, but the very idea of assessing one's reading numerically is also odd. Electing to read *A La Recherche Du Temps Perdu* in any given year would lose you Rove's contest, but gain you Proust.

And, of course, if you were inclined to consider Bush stupid, then it had to be said that the world when he left office could give you some evidence to back you up. Bush's wars in Iraq and Afghanistan still look disastrous; and the economy, as we shall see in Chapter Three, was also in a poor state. Perhaps Reaganish charm could only get you so far.

OBAMA AND HIS OPPONENTS

At any rate, from the Bush era on, there has been the recurring sense that Democrats are smart (a Republican voter might suspiciously call them 'slick') and that Republicans 'tell it like it is' (a Democratic voter might prefer to call them 'dumb').

In 2008, John McCain's campaign for the presidency continued this trend. The self-proclaimed 'maverick of the Senate' floundered throughout against the more eloquent then first-term senator Barack Obama. It was McCain's choice of Sarah Palin as his running mate which represented the sharpest decline yet in the national discourse – at least until Trump's run in 2016.[25] Palin represented an anti-intellectual streak in America. Religiosity, as distinct from true religious feeling, was a dominant note, and she expressed herself in tortuous sentences: 'I know at the end of the day putting this in God's hands, the right thing for America will be done, at the end of the day on Nov. 4',[26] being a not unrepresentative example. In Palinland, facts took a back seat. Upon no evidence, she stated that Obama was 'palling around with terrorists'. Today's Republican Party with its regular demonisations of Obama as 'un-American' sings from her hymn-sheet.

McCain's immediate punishment for choosing Palin was to lose the 2008 election, but he has also lived to see his Party become more like her, and less like him, as a result of his choice.[27]

The conclusion was becoming harder to escape: one side of the divide had become more intelligent than the other. For the 2008 cycle, this would likely always have been the case. Perhaps after eight years of Barack Obama, it's easy to forget how intelligent he is. Here was a President who ranges easily over law and science, a man also steeped in history and literature. His book *Dreams From My Father* was praised by Toni Morrison and Philip Roth. His oratory could mesh Martin Luther King Jr., Abraham Lincoln and JFK. It might be that liberals swooned too much. It is true that 'Yes, we can', though a profound rallying cry with huge historical resonance from the Cesar Chavez era, is not 'the better angels of our nature', and that Obama's speeches can lack quotability. But throughout the 2008 campaign, Obama showed a commitment to nuance. This was never more vivid than in his address 'A More Perfect Union'. Footage had surfaced of Obama's former pastor Reverend Jeremiah Wright spouting controversial views about 9/11 ('America's chickens are coming home to roost!'), but Obama refused to fight on the terrain of soundbite, and instead presented the electorate a 45-minute lecture on the issue of race in America. When in his First Inaugural Address, Obama quoted St. Paul and talked of putting away childish things, it really did seem plausible that, under his leadership, America would.

Barack Obama ran not just as the extraordinarius, but as the enlightened candidate (Figure 3). He promised a style of government based on reasonable debate flowing out of the best information he could find. Bush had famously sometimes 'gone with his gut,' as he had on the Iraq War. Obama's cerebral approach was an implicit promise that, although he might make mistakes, they would not be impulsive ones. The distinction was real, which is not to say it hasn't been exaggerated. Bush's post-presidency memoir, *Decision Points,*

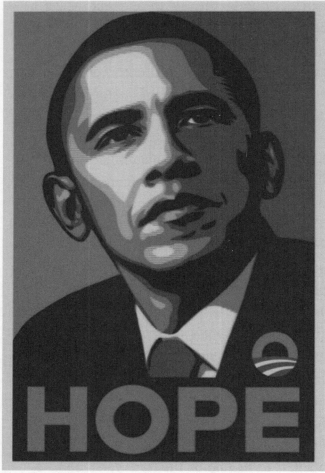

Fig 3. Barack Obama, the enlightened extraordinarius, in his 2008 campaign poster.[28]

shows that for all his failings – many of which, as in Iraq and in his slow reaction to Hurricane Katrina, were caused by an unwillingness to look at facts – Bush did grapple, far more than his detractors might expect, with minutiae. Yet Obama was effective in distancing himself from his predecessor precisely because he was describing a more or less true state of affairs. Bush had famously styled himself as the 'Decider', by which he appears to have meant that he had the ability to cut through inconvenient complexity and arrive, usually via an inspired hunch, at the heart of the matter. Obama stood in opposition to this tactic.

For Obama, if there were many sides to every question, then what was the point of partisanship? He had first come to national attention in his address to the 2004 Democratic National Convention:

> We worship an awesome God in the Blue States, and we don't like federal agents poking around in our libraries in the Red States. We coach Little League in the Blue States, and, yes, we've got some gay friends in the Red States. There are patriots who opposed the war in Iraq and there are patriots who supported the war in Iraq.

Obama in this mode reminds one a little of William James. In *The Varieties of Religious Experience*, James seeks not to prove the existence of God one way or the other, but simply to describe the human heart. Obama came before America as if he had no agenda other than to describe the world around him. This approach helped him get elected, but when it turned out that he did have an agenda after all, it upset those who had assumed his politics would be an exact match with theirs.

Not that he has ever particularly given up on the idea of being the adult intellect in the room. To this day, the President persists with a bipartisan tone, and has an admirable habit of attempting imaginative leaps into what his opponents might be thinking. A recent example of this was at a town hall on gun control where he went out of his way to understand the gun-owner mentality:

> At one point Michelle turned to me and said, 'You know, if I was living in a farmhouse where the sheriff's department is pretty far away and somebody can just turn off the highway and come up to the farm, I would want

to have a shotgun or a rifle to make sure
I was protected and to make sure my
family was protected.'[29]

What is the Obama method of governing?
He begins always with this act of imaginative
empathy: people are struggling to pay for
healthcare, or people are dying because it's
too easy to get guns. This imaginative act is
analogous to Francis Bacon's idea of 'lighting
a candle' which I quoted in the previous
chapter. Just as the scientist must decide what
experiment to attempt, the politician must
decide what problem most requires attention. It
is then Obama's custom, as we shall see in the
next chapters, to proceed along the course that
he thinks most likely to produce a reasonable
solution to that problem – he tries to 'light the
way', to continue the Bacon analogy.

　　　This will involve a deep consideration
of opposing points of view. Those inside the
administration attest that Obama prefers to
hear every voice on an issue before making his
decision. This decision-making part he always
does alone.

　　　All of which sounds like a very
enlightened – and Enlightenment – way of going

about politics. In my next few chapters I shall describe the country Obama inherited and then assess how successful the experiment has been.

But first it will be necessary to look at the Republican reaction to his presence in the White House, since that reaction altered the conditions of that experiment as surely as a beech marten in the Hadron Collider.

THE REPUBLICANS POST-2008

Throughout his 2008 campaign Obama had spoken of dysfunction in Washington, and had vowed to end it. But there was little, one suspects, Obama could have done to prepare himself for the state of affairs in 2009, reported here by Michael Grunwald three years later:

> ...the Republican plot to obstruct President Obama [began] before he even took office, including secret meetings led by House GOP whip Eric Cantor (in December 2008) and Senate minority leader Mitch McConnell (in early January 2009) in which they laid out their daring (though cynical and political) no-honeymoon strategy of all-out resistance

to a popular President-elect during an economic emergency. 'If he was for it,' former Ohio Senator George Voinovich explained, 'we had to be against it.'[30]

Obama appears to have been slow to understand that this was happening, and still seems perplexed that it happened at all: he recently opined that if he were to put forward a cure for cancer, he'd expect Republicans to oppose it. But things have only deteriorated from what at the time seemed a low point. When McConnell assumed the role of Senate Majority Leader in 2010, he wasted no time in informing *The National Journal* that: 'The single most important thing we want to achieve is for President Obama to be a one-term president.'[31]

The GOP became – in Grunwald's phrase – *The Party of No*. So far this has been a disaster for the Republicans at the presidential level. But it has had much success elsewhere: under Obama, the Democrats have lost 13 Senate seats, 69 House seats, and 12 governorships. This strategy of the Republicans' has hampered Obama, and would likely continue to hamper a President Hillary Clinton.

The achievements of the Obama administration must be read in this context:

everything that has been accomplished has been accomplished in the teeth of fierce – and usually unwarranted – opposition. The debt ceiling was raised 18 times under Ronald Reagan; under Obama it has become a regular point of contention. Obama was called a liar during a 2009 joint session of Congress by Republican Joe Wilson. He has been persuaded by Donald Trump to produce his birth certificate. When a valid document was produced, Trump failed to apologise: 'I am really honored and I am really proud, that I was able to do something that nobody else could do.' The falsehood that Obama is Kenyan still permeates the electorate. In a 2011 Gallup poll, 23% of Republicans thought Obama was 'definitely' or 'probably not' born in the US. Petulance and misinformation can sometimes appear to be winning.

But abandoning truth has had its cost. Being The Party of No is no picnic if the party you are naysaying happens to be speaking sense. This has led to some curious contortions. Republicans now fall over themselves to find the words to express their rage at the President's healthcare bill. One 2016 Republican candidate Dr Ben Carson called Obamacare worse than slavery, and many today still vilify Ohio

Governor John Kasich – the most moderate Republican in the 2016 field – for accepting the administration's increased Medicare monies, funds intended for the elderly infirm. None of the Republican candidates believes in man-made climate change. They are universally opposed – or, in Marco Rubio's case, came to be opposed – to immigration reform. Most would make severe cuts to the social safety net, and try to replace government help with a tax credit. So that while the Obama administration has been predominantly thoughtful in its approach to government, the Republican Party has been consistently contemptuous of facts and committed not to the needs of their constituents but to the wrecking of Obama's career.

If this is the case – and I believe it is incontrovertible – then to understand what is really at stake in the 2016 election, one needs to know what government undertaken according to Enlightenment principles looks like. It will tell us what we are in danger of losing in the event of a President Trump. And only by looking at policy – its detail and effects – can we bypass the media-circus brand of politics that Trump wants us to have, and look at the reality of American lives and all of our lives.

And so we must now imagine that the fanfare of Election Day 2008 is over. George W. Bush is about to retreat to his ranch and to his painting. The Obamas are about to descend on Washington D.C. for the inauguration. At venues throughout Washington D.C., the marquees are going up, and the tables are being laid. President-elect Barack Hussein Obama is about to be briefed for the first time about the state of the nation. What would his advisors be saying?

PART II

THE OBAMA ADMINISTRATION

CHAPTER 3 – THE OBAMA PREDICAMENT

Yet, every so often, the oath is taken amidst gathering clouds and raging storms.
– President Barack Obama, First Inaugural Address, 2009

Few Presidents have been dealt such a difficult hand as President Barack Obama. We would need to go back to FDR to find a comparably challenging inheritance. Many have sought to describe it, but his predecessor put it most vividly when, in his later memoir *Decision Points*, he recalled his state of mind just before handing over the reins:

> I reflected on everything we were facing. Over the past few weeks we had seen the failure of America's two largest mortgage entities, the bankruptcy of a major investment bank, the sale of another, the nationalization of the world's largest insurance company, and now the most drastic intervention in the free market since the presidency of Franklin Roosevelt. At the same time, Russia

had invaded and occupied Georgia, Hurricane Ike had hit Texas, and America was fighting a two-front war in Iraq and Afghanistan. This was one ugly way to end the presidency.[32]

Indeed it was. And Bush's exit took place among the same scenery as Obama's entrance. It is now necessary – to return to the Francis Bacon passage again – to light the candle on these problems in their detail.

THE ECONOMY WHEN OBAMA TOOK OFFICE

In the month that Obama took office, 796,000 jobs were lost. It was also the twelfth straight month of job losses. To look now at the 2008 posters of Hope and Change, showing the President's face at a visionary tilt, one might retrospectively forget the misery and the desperation in the country around the time of his election. His calm demeanour during a period of crisis convinced voters to overlook his youth. Euphoria at the election of the first black president would be brief analgesic to real economic pain.

The origins of the 2008-2009 Great Recession are still not perfectly comprehended, but any explanation would first need to contend with the housing crisis. During the 2000s, many Americans had purchased mortgage packages they either hadn't understood, or had assumed were less risky than they were. The dream of owning a house, and the economic wishful-thinking that can easily enter the mind of anyone who wants a better life, were allowed to prosper within a system of highly complex mortgages, exotically financed by mortgage-backed securities and collateralised debt obligations. When previously high prices fell, and interest rates rose, many found it impossible to refinance, and the demand for mortgage-backed securities evaporated. The crisis spread upwards, causing a bank run on the very shadow banking system which we have already seen Reagan and Clinton deregulating in the 1980s and 90s. One after the other, organisations came forward to confess that they had strayed from their tasks: Bear Stearns and Merrill Lynch, Fannie Mae and Freddie Mac, Lehman Brothers, AIG and Washington Mutual. The Lehman Brothers bankruptcy in 2008 was the largest in US history.

Added to the sense of crisis was the sense of its being a complex crisis. It was a kind of Frankenstein economy, a world of strange monsters the system had somehow created. Many had been sold mortgages by people who themselves may not have understood them – and more importantly weren't as bothered as they should have been about whether their clients could afford them. In 2007, Paul Krugman had reported Bill Gross, bond manager of Pimco, as saying: 'What we are witnessing is essentially the breakdown of our modern-day banking system, a complex of leveraged lending so hard to understand that Federal Reserve Chairman Ben Bernanke required a face-to-face refresher course from hedge fund managers in mid-August.'[33] Suddenly in 2007-2008, the newspapers began to run explainers on what a sub-prime mortgage was, and no doubt some who confusedly scanned those reports had already bought their own package on the expectation of attractive rates of return and were suffering the consequences. The banks asked first Bush, then Obama, for help. Mismanagement had drifted up through the system to land on two presidents' desks. The Financial Crisis Enquiry Commission would later state in sober prose:

When borrowers stopped making
mortgage payments, the losses —
amplified by derivatives — rushed
through the pipeline. As it turned out,
these losses were concentrated in a
set of systemically important financial
institutions....Too many of these
institutions acted recklessly, taking on
too much risk....[34]

Few things are more annoying than to be duped
financially by someone richer than you are who
doesn't need the money. Who can say in what
numbers anger and resentment in 2009 may have
resurfaced as Trumpism or as #feelthebern in
2016? Alan Greenspan, Chairman of the Federal
Reserve from 1987 until 2006 would later tell
a Congressional hearing that he had made a
mistake in assuming that banks could regulate
themselves. He had, but he himself still owned
a big house. Ben Bernanke, who was Chairman
at the time of the crash, was reappointed
by President Obama against protests from
Obama's own camp.[35] These were figures from
the Reagan era, who espoused a sort of faith in
the free market which, as Obama took the oath
of office, had come to seem dangerously out-of-

date. It is one of the paradoxes of the period that at the precise time when Reagan-style policies were exposed, the popularity of Reagan himself had never been higher: a clear indication of the disjunction in politics between personality and policy.

On top of the banking crisis, Obama also had an ailing auto industry on his plate. Car manufacturers had experienced a squeeze in the mid to late 2000s. In effect people worldwide had been buying more and more Toyotas and fewer Fords and Chryslers. The industry was vulnerable to recession, and recession came. Those who had lost their homes understandably didn't want to go out and buy cars, and in any case, those who did were more likely to purchase those which met fuel-efficiency standards, and US companies had been remarkably stubborn in refusing to make such cars. Ford had obtained a line of credit in 2007. Bailouts of Chrysler and General Motors had been set in motion during the dying days of the Bush administration, but it would be up to Obama to decide how to proceed. The expectation was that the closing down of the automobile industry would lose the economy a further 3,000 jobs at a time when it couldn't afford to lose them.

The economic meltdown caused many Americans to reach the conclusion that the problem wasn't establishment Republicans or establishment Democrats: the problem had become the establishment, right and left. The Democratic Party base, of course, could be relied-upon not to love Wall Street. But this time around, the Republican voter began to wonder whether the platform of his party – tax cuts for the very people who had engendered the recession, and a limited social safety net for them – was really what they were after. Reaganomics looks especially hard-hearted when the economy isn't doing well. Anger already percolated. We now know that many were becoming open to extreme solutions.

So as Obama stood in the cold and began his first Inaugural Address (Figure 4) with the words I quoted at the top of this chapter, the recession jockeyed with the historic nature of the moment to take the uppermost position in people's minds. The nation had a black president, yes, but it also had falling stock prices, house prices down 30%, and foreclosures up 81% for 2008. We tend to struggle to imagine those traits we least possess, and Obama, the calm man, now presided over an angry people:

that juxtaposition would not always turn out well for him.

McConnell and Cantor got their wish. Obama never had a honeymoon period.

Fig 4. Obama's First Inauguration. "Obama, the calm man, now presided over an angry people: that juxtaposition would not always turn out well for him." [36]

Fig 5. In the coming years, the above would be a common sight.[37]

THE HEALTHCARE SYSTEM IN 2008

As important as the economy was in everybody's minds, the President had already told his inner circle that he had bigger plans than just fixing the immediate problem. In a recent article for *Politico*, Michael Grunwald tells the following story:

> Early in his presidential transition, Obama led a brainstorming session with his policy team about first-term accomplishments. [Timothy] Geithner [Secretary of the Treasury] offered a downer of a reality check: 'Your accomplishment is going to be preventing a second Great Depression.'
>
> 'That's not enough for me,' the president-elect shot back. 'I'm not going to be defined by what I prevented.'[38]

By which he meant, among other things, healthcare reform.

Obamacare, like the financial crisis, looms over the 2016 election. It is worth remembering what it was originally meant to address. Put simply, by the end of the Bush administration, around 45 million Americans had no access to health insurance. The idea of universal healthcare in the US had been a hot-button issue for liberals, and numerous presidents, Democrat and Republican, as far back as Theodore Roosevelt, who had been the first to endorse the idea as a candidate for the Bull Moose Party in 1912. It had been left undone even by great reforming presidents like FDR and Lyndon Johnson, both of whom managed to accomplish so much else. Truman, Nixon and Clinton had directed much energy toward it, and the most recent attempt to get something passed had been scarring for liberals. Upon assuming office in 1993, President Clinton had charged Hillary Clinton as First Lady with the task of drawing up a healthcare plan. Clinton had envisaged a system in which insurance would be provided by employers. Republicans opposed it and proposed instead the idea of an individual mandate.[39] The Clinton administration did successfully rebound to pass the State Children's Health Insurance Program, a program whose expansion George W. Bush would later veto, but the idea of universal healthcare was once again on hold.

At the time of his inauguration, Obama may not have guessed that by putting forward a system based around the individual mandate, a Republican idea first introduced in Mitt Romney's state of Massachusetts, he would shortly incur the wrath of those who had proposed it.[40] The injustice of the present system was uppermost in his mind. In the coming years he would turn repeatedly to the memory of his mother who had died of uterine and ovarian cancer:

> She was 52 years old and...you know what she was thinking about in the last months of her life? She wasn't thinking about getting well. She wasn't thinking about coming to terms with her own mortality. She had been diagnosed just as she was transitioning between jobs. And she wasn't sure whether insurance was going to cover the medical expenses because they might consider this a pre-existing condition. I remember just being heartbroken, seeing her struggle through the paperwork and the medical bills and the insurance forms. So, I have seen what it's like when somebody you love is

suffering because of a broken health care system. And it's wrong. It's not who we are as a people.[41]

It is worth remembering this story when we come to describe the steadfast and angry opposition to Obamacare: whatever its faults as legislation, it would be a hard-hearted person who felt there was anything other than moral urgency behind the decision to pursue it. And yet in 2016, Republicans candidates talk as if the healthcare bill had been specifically designed to irritate them.

But if the President's own story, reiterated on the campaign trail and subject of a campaign ad 'Mother', was not enough for some people, there would have been plenty of others to choose from. In 2009, Ed Pilkington of *The Guardian* would visit Kansas and report back in an article 'Dying for Affordable Healthcare –The Uninsured Speak.' The piece tells the story of gynaecologist Dr. Joseph Manley who in the late 1980s began experiencing involuntary muscle movements and difficulty swallowing. Pilkington writes:

He remained uninsured and largely untreated for his progressively severe condition for the following 11 years. Blood tests that could have diagnosed him correctly were not done because he couldn't afford the $200. Having lost his practice, he lost his mansion on the hill and now lives in a one-bedroom apartment in the suburbs. His Porsches have made way for bangers. Many times this erstwhile pillar of the medical establishment had to go without food in order to pay for basic medicines. In 2000 Manley finally found the help he needed, at a clinic in Kansas City that acts as a rare safety net for uninsured people. He was swiftly diagnosed with Huntington's disease, a degenerative genetic illness, and now receives regular medical attention through the clinic.

When Obama took office, the uninsured were vulnerable even at the higher end of society. But Manley's story, moving as it is, is not representative – such safety nets were, alas, all too rare. Those with less money were more likely to have their lives cut short: an unacceptable state of affairs for a country that could apparently afford to act as the world's policeman, and put money towards space travel.

President Bush had opined that the talk of universal healthcare was unnecessary: 'After all, you just go to an emergency room.' This suggested a fundamental ignorance: Bush's attitude overlooked the importance of ongoing care in people's lives. Many would leave that suspicious-looking growth, or overlook the last few weeks' curious tiredness, in the hope of making savings. Those with 'pre-existing conditions' were repeatedly denied insurance coverage. The cost of health insurance had become a major economic issue in itself: the US spent – and still spends under Obama – more on healthcare per capita than does any other developed country.

In both the financial situation and in these deficiencies in the healthcare system, an Enlightenment ideal was under threat. We have seen how the Declaration of Independence had framed the matter in terms of the pursuit of happiness for all. Neither is the preamble to The Constitution silent on the matter:

We the people of the United States, in order to form a more perfect Union, establish justice, insure domestic tranquility, provide for the common defense, promote the general welfare, and secure the blessings of liberty to ourselves and our posterity, do ordain and establish this Constitution for the United States of America.

'The general welfare' was not provided for. It is true that for many libertarians the spectre of government healthcare would have then seemed – as it seems now – an infraction on 'the blessings of liberty'. But the distinction between the right to life, and the right not to have a small amount of liberty infringed upon, was a valid one for the majority of Americans: according to a 2008 poll in *The New York Times*, 62% of the country felt the Democrat pledge for universal healthcare was the right one, while only 24% were satisfied with Bush's handling of the nation's healthcare system.

IN THE SITUATION ROOM

2008 was an election about the state of the economy, but it was also a foreign policy election.

As we saw in Chapter Two, President Bush's response to the September 11th attacks had initially been popular enough for Democrats to rally around. Afghanistan had been invaded and the Taliban seemingly routed. Bush had visibly enjoyed articulating the Manichean nature of the fight, and his poll numbers had risen. But he had overestimated the possibilities of American military power, and had overlooked the tribal complexity of the countries he had invaded. Over time, his cowboyish approach would create deep division in American society. The decision to invade Iraq in 2003 loomed larger over the 2008 election than one tends to remember now that the country is just one of many items on the news. It might have had fewer detractors had it been conducted according to purely humanitarian arguments. What most rankled for Democrats was the claim, made by Colin Powell in his February 2003 presentation to the United Nations, that the Hussein regime was deliberately hiding weapons of mass destruction from UN weapons inspectors. Powell would later express his regret about his own involvement in the case for war.

The invasion dragged on and the world sobered up, to Bush's disadvantage. Saddam

Hussein – bearded and confused – was found hiding in a spider-hole near his home town of Tikrit, and there was only passing jubilation. Dick Cheney, Bush's Vice-President, and Donald Rumsfeld, his Defence Secretary, had promised 'shock and awe' – a thrilling exhibition of American military might in the deserts. Instead Americans had ended up listening to Rumsfeld's vague and surreal explanations about Saddam Hussein's lack of weapons of mass destruction:

> Reports that say that something hasn't happened are always interesting to me, because as we know, there are known knowns; there are things we know we know. We also know there are known unknowns; that is to say we know there are some things we do not know. But there are also unknown unknowns – the ones we don't know we don't know. And if one looks throughout the history of our country and other free countries, it is the latter category that tend to be the difficult ones. [42]

It was a vivid insight into a confused administration. Osama bin Laden had not been found. Obama had vowed to redouble American efforts to locate him. His long record of opposing the intervention – contrasted with Hillary Clinton's 2003 vote in favour – was the principal reason why he had won his party's nomination, and a major reason for his winning the presidency. Anything besides a major recalibration of American foreign policy would have been tantamount to a violation of his campaign.

What was the situation on the ground? By 2008, Iraq, in spite of the seeming success of the 2006 'surge' in troops, had an extremely dilapidated infrastructure. In the aftermath of the invasion, Bush and UK Prime Minister Tony Blair were guilty of a cardinal sin among statesmen: they had failed to give the world their detailed attention. John Robertson in his recent book on the country, after surveying thousands of years of rich Iraqi history, arrives at the Bush era with the following description:

> Except in the Kurdish region, where the US had been perceived as a liberator as early as the 1990s, almost from the beginning the invasion spawned insurgency against the occupation across

the country, especially in the so-called "Sunni Triangle" around Baghdad and in the Anbar region of western Iraq – notably in the city of Fallujah, which US forces devastated in 2004 – and also in the Shi'ite south, where a militia (the "Mahdi Army") affiliated with the young mullah Muqtada al-Sadr (son of the Ayatollah Muhammad Sadiq al-Sadr) battled the Americans in and around Najaf. That insurgency was stoked by an ill-advised decision by L. Paul Bremer, the American proconsul installed after the coalition's takeover, to disband the Iraqi army and outlaw the Baath Party.[43]

Obama had criticised the original invasion as loudly as anyone, but now all these problems were on his desk. To the complexities Robertson describes might be added the outrage of torture. The 2003 publication of pictures from Abu-Ghraib prison had depicted American soldiers mocking Iraqi captives. The images retain the power to scandalise. The image of prisoner, Ali Shallal Al-Qaisi, hooded in a kind of black Ku Klux Klan hat, his fingers plugged into electrodes, was beamed round the world (Figure

6). There were also photographs of army reserve soldier Lynndie England. In one she is shown thumbs-upping over a pyramid of naked Iraqi bodies. In another she holds a leash tied round the neck of a writhing captive (Figure 7). The photos illustrate more vividly than any statistic could the moral repugnancy of the times.

Fig 6. Abu Graib. This is Ali Shallal Al-Qaisi, and those are electrodes tied to his fingers. The photo illustrates the shame of the Bush years.[44]

Fig 7. This is army reserve soldier Lynndie England, another appalling image to come out of Abu Graib. Donald Trump has vowed to do much worse.[45]

And none of this, miserable as it was, was free. The cost of the war is difficult to project even now, with billions of dollars in benefits still owed to veterans, and interest payments unpredictable, but by 2013, the Costs of War Project, conducted by the Watson Institute for International Studies at Brown University, had identified costs of $1.7 trillion with a projected overall cost somewhere in the region of $6 trillion.

It is worth asking what America got for its money. It is true that a brutal dictator was removed and that elections were held. But these gains never really stacked up against the loss of life. By 2013, it was estimated that 134,000 Iraqi civilians were killed together with an additional death toll for aid workers, journalists, security forces and insurgents totalling somewhere between 42,000 and 55,000.[46] A grimmer ten-year anniversary is hard to imagine. But when Obama took office, the cost of the war and the thought that it had been waged for no decent reason were problems compounding and mutually reinforcing one another, adding to a sense of overall anxiety. Obama in 2009 could not have known how high these estimates would run (although his 2008 campaign stump speeches showed the cost of the war was very much on his mind) but he would have seen the report by the 2007 Congressional Budget for Responsibility, which stated that the US wars in Iraq and Afghanistan could cost taxpayers a total of $2.4 trillion by 2017.[47]

President Bush had left even more international difficulties for Obama. Confronted with a variety of hatreds, Bush had preferred to lump them together as one. It is, for instance, noteworthy how widely the destinies of the countries in Bush's so-called Axis of Evil have diverged since the 2002 State of Union in which he coined that term. Iran is now tentatively part of the international community. Iraq, as a result of the invasion, is hardly a state at all. North Korea gains regular media coverage on account of its apparent closeness to the development of a nuclear weapon, but it has an undeniable eccentricity stemming from the caprices of its dictator Kim Jong-Un. But then each case was always different, and to pretend otherwise had been to attempt to simplify a complicated world. In 2008, uppermost in Obama's mind was the possibility of rapprochement with Iran, a country which Obama didn't see as – to use Bush's word – 'evil,' but as a country with a young population which might have an interest in opening relations. When the new President said on the day of his inauguration: 'To the Muslim world, we seek a new way forward, based on mutual interest and mutual respect', he was addressing young Iranians as much as anyone. Furthermore, at the time Obama assumed office, the shape of American foreign policy was questionable: an American president would typically spend a huge amount of time on the Middle East, both in war and in supporting a sometimes dubious clientele (Egypt, Saudi Arabia), and very little time in developing relationships with Asia and South America. Meanwhile small countries, like Cuba, had no diplomatic relations with the US, even though they posed no immediate threat.

In retrospect we can also see that other difficulties were quietly developing. The people of Egypt, Libya, Tunisia and Syria were all becoming tired of life under their various autocratic regimes. The death of the militant Abu Musab Al-Zarqawi in 2006 had left behind more of a legacy than anyone had supposed: if Al-Qaeda were to be defeated, then we now know that an even more virulent strain of radical fundamentalism would be there to take its stead. A posturing and imperialist Russia, led by Vladimir Putin, was very much known to Obama, but it couldn't be known that oil prices were about to fall, rendering him still more unpredictable over the next eight years.

Most worryingly of all, there was the need to orchestrate all these disparate elements – both the more or less entrenched problems, and whatever additional problems might come along – into a greener world economy.

RISING SEAS, WARMING TEMPERATURES

Over the late 1900s and early 2000s, climate scientists had become increasingly troubled by trends in the planet. The heat-trapping nature of carbon dioxide had been noted as early as the mid-19th century, alongside the observation that humankind, newly industrialised, had taken to releasing a large amount of it into the atmosphere. The scientific community had long collected data on sea levels, and had begun to notice alarming rises. Coastal tide gauge and satellite records show sea levels had risen from 1880 measurements by about two inches at the time of the Roosevelt administration, and by as much as eight inches when Obama took office. The planet as a whole had also warmed noticeably in the 40 or so years before Obama took office. This had also been closely linked to warmer oceans, diminished ice sheets, more acidic oceans and less snow, all with catastrophic results for the diversity of life. The political world had been alerted to these facts. The 2007 Intergovernmental Panel on Climate Change Fourth Assessment Report had found a greater than 90% likelihood that humans were responsible for these changes to climate. In the UK, the Stern Review on the Economics of Climate Change had seconded these findings, but had also placed emphasis on the missed economic opportunity of tackling the problem.

An international orthodoxy had emerged in every place except America.

Today the Republican Party is the only major political party in the world to deny climate change. To imagine what the world's energy policy would be like under any of the 2016 Republican candidates, it is necessary to look at the Bush administration's record.

In the first instance, the Bush administration refused to ratify the Kyoto Protocols which would have required all countries to reduce their carbon emissions. Vice-President Dick Cheney had explained: 'You can't shut down the world economy in the name of trying to eliminate greenhouse gases.'[48] It would be business as usual. Except this wasn't a do-nothing policy. The book *Hell and High Water,* by former US Department of Energy official Joseph J. Romm, outlines the campaign which the Bush administration made to convince the public that the science was inaccurate. They argued that 'magic cures' like hydrogen cars would salvage the situation: it was an argument to continue with a high-carbon economy, and rather akin to someone receiving a diagnosis of heart trouble and continuing to drink and smoke. Cheney claimed the science was blurry, which it wasn't: it was becoming more substantial all the time, and tending only in one direction. But he also claimed that there was no imaginable business case for a green economy. By the time Obama took office, solar PV prices were hovering near $8 per watt; it was the image of an industry in its infancy. To glimpse Cheney's folly one must fast-forward. Years later, the great science writer Tim Flannery would write in *Atmosphere of Hope:*

> It is extraordinary to see how far wind and solar power have come over the past decade.... An important reason for the massive growth in wind and solar is declining cost. The manufacturers of solar panels have cut production costs by more than 80 per cent in the past five years, and efficiencies throughout the production and installation supply chain are driving costs down even further. Installers, for example, no longer have to pay a visit to quote for a job.[49]

The detail of this situation Cheney couldn't have imagined, but the suspicion remains that he should have been open to the possibility. There was also the suspicion that the administration's policy on climate change sat alongside a more widespread anti-science agenda. The Bush administration espoused the teaching of intelligent design alongside evolution as a competing theory, and restricted federal funding for research on stem cells obtained from human embryos.

Obama took office pledging, in a sometimes mocked section of his nomination victory speech in St. Paul, that his election would be looked upon as the moment when the warming of the oceans began to slow and the planet began to heal.

The difficulty he faced here, aside from opposition from Republicans at home, and persuading the Chinese to take the problem seriously, would be handling the leaders of third-world polluters such as India and Brazil, whose people were – and still in many cases are – without decent access to food, water and electricity. Bush, of course, had been spared needing to worry about such matters by disavowing climate change in the first place. But they were unavoidable for Obama.

OTHER ANXIETIES

Those were the issues uppermost in the minds
of most who watched the Obama inauguration.
But there were many others of huge importance
to many, and which would gradually attain
greater importance as other problems began
to be dealt with – or simply, as in the case of
healthcare, mutate via a projected solution, into
bitter controversy.

Same-sex marriage was still deemed
unconstitutional and had been opposed by Bush.
The Clinton-era policy of 'Don't Ask, Don't Tell'
was still the law of the land; transgender rights
were rarely discussed. Immigration, as it had
become in so many European countries, was an
emotional issue, causing anxiety among white
Americans, and a sense of unjust exclusion
among Latinos (that issue shall be looked at in
more detail in Chapter Four). The Patriot Act,
passed in the wake of the 9/11 attacks, had
radically increased the powers of the federal
government, and though the world did not yet
know the name, a young computer professional
Edward Snowden was about to start work for
Booz Allen Hamilton as a sub-contractor to
the National Security Administration as a

cyber-strategist: as the world knows, he would not like what he discovered there. Gun crime also remained high, legally buttressed by the Second Amendment and with the existing state of the law guaranteed by a powerful gun lobby. Incarceration among African Americans had risen exponentially under Clinton and remained high.

Like this, Bush limped towards the finishing line and has ever afterwards – painting portraits and self-portraits in Texas – radiated a sense of relief that the presidency was off his shoulders. His achievements – chief among them the increase of AIDS monies to Africa, and perhaps the Troubled Asset Relief Program (see Chapter Four) – unfortunately feel a little thin on the ground.

That was the predicament. What Obama said on Inauguration Day was not, in fact, especially memorable. The historian Simon Schama criticised it as rather cold – and indeed it lacked the poetry of Abraham Lincoln's great addresses, or even any of the catchy oratorical tropes of an FDR or a Kennedy. But in a curious way disappointment at this lapse in oratory had its own story to tell: it was time to get to work.

CHAPTER 4 – WHAT THE ADMINISTRATION DID

Never let a crisis go to waste.

– Rahm Emanuel, Chief of Staff to President Barack Obama 2009-2011

Eloquence in politics can be double-edged. It can inspire people, but also leave them deflated when policy is wrangled over and the mess of government commences. The division between what seemed possible and what turned out to be achievable has rarely been so large as with the Obama administration – but this doesn't mean that a great deal hasn't been achieved. The loftiness of Obama's rhetoric was thrown into relief by the compromises of politics. When asked to name a regret towards the end of his presidency, Obama often says that he failed at the outset to communicate the busyness of his administration – a classic politician's tactic of admitting to a weakness by hinting at a strength.

But this self-rebuke isn't empty modesty; there's truth to it. In early 2009, many noted that the influx of e-mails which had come their way on a daily basis during the campaign had dried up now that the administration had begun. In retrospect there could have been no worse time to suspend communications with the Democratic base. As we saw in Chapter Two, Republican obstructionism rushed in to fill that void, and although it caused problems for Republicans – their defeat in the 2012 presidential election can be partly attributed to it – it also struck rightaway at the *raison d'être* of the Obama presidency. The other aspect of Obama's 'regret' was also true: Obama was, and is, an extremely active president. Sometimes the truth about an administration can be delivered to you in a chance overheard remark. Here is Jon Favreau, Obama's first-term speechwriter, speaking about those heady first 100 days:

> People were always saying: 'Why aren't we talking about this cool accomplishment? Under Clinton we would've bragged about it for weeks!' The answer was usually: 'Because there are a million other things going on.'[50]

Hyperactivity created a vacuum of communications. Obama has never satisfactorily reseized that terrain. In the 2016 election, the electorate will, as is usual, ask the question: 'Did Americans like what he did?' But they will also give a verdict on how much they minded this early breakdown of communications.

THE ECONOMY

The economy was the first thing to tackle. Since the Great Depression had struck in 1929, economists had been struggling to understand how best to cope with contractions in economies. John Maynard Keynes had provided a plausible roadmap, stating that in a recession the government should increase public spending in order to make up for a deficit in private expenditure. Many – including Bush in 2008 – have found that the Keynesian view of life with its emphasis on stimulus, looks especially compelling in an economic crisis – it at least gives governments something to do. Whereas to hold, as supply-side economists prefer, that the economy is generally in a state of equilibrium is more easily done during an up-turn in the business cycle. Certainly amid massive job losses and the prospect of a run on the shadow banking system, the market hadn't looked especially equilibrious to Bush: Adam Smith's invisible hand must have seemed very invisible then. The administration had placed Fannie Mae and Freddie Mac into conservatorship in September 2008, and then signed the Troubled Asset Relief Program the following month. Assets and equity in financial institutions had been bought up. Bailout money went to Citigroup ($45 billion), Bank of America ($45 billion) and AIG ($40 billion) to name only a few. It was a betrayal of conservative purity, but probably the right thing to do.

How exactly is stimulus meant to work? The idea is that government expenditure will put money in people's pockets to put towards consumer goods. In Keynes, the market shouldn't be left to self-correct, because it cannot self-correct. And indeed certain commonplaces of the neo-classical model – for instance that unemployment is caused by laziness – can look rather odd during financial crises: the loss of 800,000 jobs in a month would, for instance, constitute a remarkable outbreak of sloth. This is not to say that Obama was faced with a straightforward decision. The Keynesian system as a whole had experienced years of reversal in the 1980s and 90s, and there were vociferous voices arguing that deficit spending would skyrocket interest rates. In the event, this didn't happen: interest rates would instead fall.

The decision to implement a stimulus package – The American Recovery and Reinvestment Act of 2009 – brought back a school of economics that had become outmoded. Paul Krugman, the Nobel Prize-winning economist, and the most widely read writer on economic matters today, was instrumental in making the size of the stimulus package an issue for debate. At the time of the bill's passage, it had a projected cost of $787 billion; that would later be revised upwards to $831 billion. This was larger in real dollars than the New Deal, and yet because of the disappointment of Krugman and others (Krugman called it 'too little of a good thing'), the perception among the left remains that it was in some sense a cautious measure. As a piece of legislation it had the virtue of clarity: to create jobs and to assist those who had been hit by the recession.

It is difficult to assess the benefits of any one piece of financial legislation, since economics feeds, and is fed, by everything else, and so as Krugman would say: 'it's hard to disentangle the effects of the Recovery Act from all the other things that were going on at the time.'[51] Economics is also continually up against the difficulty that people's behaviour when it comes to money is often mysterious: it will probably eventually become a branch of neuroscience and is somewhat in infancy.

Nevertheless there are estimates based on thorough research of the legislation's efficacy that are worth quoting. Moody's and IHS Global Insight estimated that the stimulus saved or created 1.6 to 1.8 million jobs and forecast a total impact of 2.5 million jobs saved. The Congressional Budget Office felt that this estimate was conservative, and plumped for a figure of 2.1 million jobs in the last quarter of 2009 alone. A 2012 IGM Forum poll conducted by the University of Chicago's Booth School of Business found that 80% of leading economists agree unemployment was lower at the end of 2010 than it would have been without the stimulus.[52] Ted Cruz's subsequent suggestion in a 2016 presidential debate that the system would have been better off left to itself, and that Mom and Pop (not Wall Street) should have been bailed out, must answer to the fact that many ordinary people *were* bailed out. This was especially the case if you happened to be a teacher: the aid went to state and local governments, and education budgets would have been particularly hurt without the stimulus money.

But this was far from all that the legislation did: in fact, it reshaped the priorities of the US economy. Its aid was weighted towards the vulnerable, and an estimated 13 million Americans were lifted out of poverty as a result. It also sponsored numerous hard-hat projects that upgraded 42,000 miles of road, 2,700 bridges and 6,000 miles of rail. The package also included roughly $300 billion worth of tax cuts for businesses and families.[53] It was a highly progressive piece of legislation. For the first time, an urgent commitment to tackle climate change entered the finances of the US: the Recovery Act did an enormous amount to nudge the economy in the direction of clean energy. It also moved the healthcare system into the digital age.

The legislation provides a window into Obama's governing style, both as to its scale – as big as it could be, but not so big that it wouldn't pass – and as to its hodgepodge and messy feel – last-minute Republican-senator demands were met in order to avoid a filibuster. This pattern would be repeated, and so it is worth looking at. Obama is always eager for bipartisanship at first, but will plough ahead once he realises cooperation isn't possible.

The initial period of seeking support can seem, and usually is, a straight waste of time, but it does enable him to project the impression (usually a true one) that he has exhausted all the possibilities of cooperation. What he is aiming for always needs to be big – one of his favourite words is 'historic' – but his ambitions must be rooted in reality, which might mean compromise. But any concession he makes will be met with the oft-repeated mantra: 'I'll handle the politics.' He has always trusted his own charisma to smooth defects in policy. Untidiness must not be permitted to impinge on 'getting things done'.

The 2016 election is in part an experiment in what people will feel about his policies when he isn't so much around. And 2020, particularly if a Democrat wins in November, may be an election about how Americans feel about the America he has built when he's hardly there at all.

THE PIVOT TO OBAMACARE

The provisions within the Recovery Act to digitalise medicine look in retrospect like a signal to the electorate and to his enemies: I am serious about healthcare.

In his first 100 days, Obama had already signed into law an expanded State Children's Health Insurance Program, an opening salvo which insured another four million children. He also moved to secure a congressional budget resolution to enact major healthcare reform. All along, Obama had faced a choice – to govern 'small ball', as Clinton had done, or to risk larger schemes. He had made up his mind: healthcare would proceed. He had campaigned on the idea of creating a government-run health insurance agency – the so-called 'public option' – and had opposed the idea of an individual mandate. The public option would die hard. Here is Obama on July 18th, 2009:

> Any plan I sign must include an insurance exchange – a one-stop-shopping marketplace where you can compare the benefits, costs and track records of a variety of plans, including a public option to increase competition and keep insurance companies honest...[54]

But soon Obama back-tracked and called this 'one sliver' of his overall plan. The administration had concluded that it didn't have support for a regulated public exchange, which would have been a necessary step towards the single-payer plan which Bernie Sanders would espouse in 2016. He concluded that it would be better to press ahead with a mandate-based reform plan, which would also prohibit insurers from denying coverage on the basis of pre-existing conditions, and provide subsidies to those who could not afford the mandate. Meanwhile Medicaid would be expanded and Medicare restructured.

What followed was miserably complex, and wearying for all. 60 votes were needed to pass the bill in the Senate. Moderate Democrats needed to be appeased, and the bill was in continual flux to meet these objections. Then in August 2009, the leonine Ted Kennedy, a long-time proponent of healthcare reform, died, potentially depriving Democrats of an expected vote. Hopes for Republican cooperation on a Republican idea gradually folded: Obama's enemies doubled down on petulance and misinformation. There was talk of 'death panels',[55] and the word 'unconstitutional' was bandied about by Republicans.[56]

Muddy and drawn-out as the process was, it was merely democracy in action. The

Founding Fathers had envisaged separation of powers, and this was it. But freedom of speech can sometimes be freedom to spout misinformation. And so it happened in this instance: shrill claims of 'government takeover' had their effect, and Obama, though he tried to coin the phrase a 'New Foundation' to describe what he was doing, never quite seized the initiative. On February 4th of 2010, an electoral earthquake ensued: Republican Scott Brown won Kennedy's seat in Massachusetts.[57] At this point, Obama faced a definite fork in the road – to take the advice of his Chief of Staff Rahm Emanuel and plump for a smaller bill, or to press on. Obama chose the latter, and it took a piece of cunning to push it through: a Senate bill had already been passed, and without a full majority, the administration – helped by the House Speaker Nancy Pelosi – took it up again, and managed to push it through the House of Representatives by a process known as reconciliation. It could hardly have been uglier, and Republicans fumed. The extent of the rage pointed to the size of the achievement: Vice President Joe Biden was right when he called it 'a big fucking deal'. By the final quarter of 2015, the uninsured rate had plunged from 18%

to 11.4%. As of September 2015, 17.6 million had enrolled. Costs have continued to come in below predictions.

Twice, then, Obama had secured an enormous legislative victory while also managing to seem as though he'd done something mediocre and vaguely unpleasant. Had all those stadium speeches created hubris, and made him feel he didn't need to communicate what he was doing, that the chants of *O-ba-ma* would always be there for him? Was it just an inevitable falling-off that all modern presidents, governing in prose, will experience? Can soaring rhetoric ever be matched by political deed? Or was it a specifically media-driven injustice, the largeness of the achievement somehow obscured by reportage on the day-to-day squabbles of the legislative process? Whatever the cause – and all these factors were likely involved – Obamacare is vital to understanding the dynamics of the 2016 race. Those who felt Obama was too cautious and should have at least secured a public option as a step towards a 'single-payer plan' have resurfaced in this election as supporters of Bernie Sanders. Those who feel broadly satisfied with the policy have Hillary Clinton as its defender. Meanwhile those alarmed by the expansion in the size of government can be found contributing to a radicalisation and an atmosphere of anger in the Republican Party.

REGULATING WALL STREET

Obama had achieved much, but he had lost control of the narrative. It didn't help that the Dodd-Frank reforms, designed to reform Wall Street, pursued the same trend: it was a hat-trick of achievement which looked like watered-down compromise to many Democrats, and like a government takeover to those on the right. To this day, Obama hasn't produced a piece of legislation that has been loved like, say, the New Deal or Lyndon Johnson's Great Society.

Wall Street reform was made urgent politically by the rescue package: it was politically unviable to win the presidency on the back of small donations, as Obama had done, and then to govern against the interests of the very people who had put him there. The Dodd-Frank reforms constitute the biggest overhaul of the financial system since the first Roosevelt administration. It worked to end the idea of the bank that was 'too big to fail' – a phrase which in itself does much to encapsulate the rage that came out of the Great Recession. Dodd-Frank also brought into being Elizabeth Warren's idea of a Consumer Financial Protection Bureau, which today is highly active on behalf of consumers and has, for instance, successfully cracked down on billions of dollars in excessive overdraft fees.

Again, the left found it inadequate. Again Republicans voted unanimously against it: the US Chamber of Commerce spent more than $1.3 billion in attempts to stymie its introduction.[58] For Wall Street, the legislation impinged on a freedom which it had grown used to, and which it had expected to retain: the reforms gave the government the right to bail out banks while also refusing stockholder rewards. The world may yet have cause to be grateful for Dodd-Frank: in early 2016, the world has suffered several financial shocks, mainly emanating out of slowed growth in the Chinese economy. By stipulating that banks should have reasonably high capital requirements, an important safeguard during future crises has hopefully been created. Furthermore, the Government Accountability Office recently found that large banks are no longer able to borrow at more advantageous rates than smaller lenders.[59] The reforms remain contentious. They are predictably loathed by the right, but on the left, major as it is, Dodd-Frank has failed to capture people's imaginations. Bernie Sanders was able to run on the idea of breaking up the banks, as if nothing has been done in this direction. In fact, Dodd-Frank gives the Fed incentives to shrink banks, and most banks have been shrinking under pressure of the new regulation. Hillary Clinton drily points out that Sanders campaigns as though Dodd-Frank never happened.

The crisis in the auto industry was, however, handled with something rare in modern politics: unequivocal success. Obama had to undergo a primer on this complex industry: presidents are always undergoing crash courses before they can even know what the issues are, let alone make decisions. Governing must sometimes feel like one big exam. After studying the state of the car companies, Obama decided on a bailout, stating in his 2009 speech to a joint session of Congress that:

> We should not, and will not, protect them [Ford, General Motors and Chrysler] from their own bad practices. But we

are committed to the goal of a re-tooled, re-imagined auto industry that can compete and win. Millions of jobs depend on it. Scores of communities depend on it. And I believe the nation that invented the automobile cannot walk from it.

It might not be strictly correct to say that America invented the car – it is a weakness of Obama's to seek to tie the world in feel-good rhetorical bows like this – but Obama was true to his word in all other respects.

The administration drove a hard bargain. It initially rejected restructuring plans from General Motors and Chrysler – loans were provided to Chrysler on condition that it enter an alliance with Fiat. It has since returned $10.6 billion to the US Treasury and the auto industry as a whole has created some 115,000 jobs. It was so much of a success story that Joe Biden incorporated it into a campaign slogan in 2012: 'Osama bin Laden is dead, but General Motors is alive.'

CONSEQUENCES OF A SHELLACKING

John Updike once complained that he sometimes received reviews berating him for the novel he didn't write. Obama has received similar notices for his administration: the decision to pursue healthcare took up an enormous amount of time which, critics argue, might have been better spent on other issues. It is particularly tempting to imagine an alternative presidency with regard to two areas – immigration and climate change. These problems, which might have been tackled legislatively, Obama has ended up tackling by executive action.

Part of the problem is that Obama felt he had more time governing alone than he did. In the mid-term elections, in 2010, the Democrats experienced what the President called a 'shellacking', surrendering the House of Representatives to a Republican Party energised by its strongly anti-government Tea Party component. From that moment on, major legislation would be difficult. When the President today talks of his regret that he didn't do more to communicate his first-term agenda, he is really lamenting the legislative inaction which flowed out of this defeat: he has only controlled a compliant government for the brief period from 20th January 2009 until November 2nd 2010.

Why did the Democrats lose in 2010? In the first place, Obama didn't get much credit for what he had prevented: Americans looked at the Recovery Act, found it hadn't much improved their pay-packets, and rendered their verdicts accordingly. In the second place, G.O.P. obstructionism worked. The electorate didn't see the childishness of Republican lawmakers, so much as exactly the kind of mess the President had promised to prevent. He had dampened expectations as President-elect much less vividly than he had stoked them as a candidate. Mid-term elections are never easy for the governing party, and Republicans, with their loyal base, have tended in recent years to do better in elections when fewer people are watching. The 2008 Obama coalition of college-educated whites, blacks and Latinos would come out and vote for him again in 2012, ensuring his re-election, but they didn't show up in 2010, or in 2014, when the Senate was surrendered. Each mid-term win has damaged Obama, but they may have also increased Republican Party hubris: the rise of Trump in 2016 has in part been made possible by the fact that the party establishment has mistaken mere protest wins for whole-hearted endorsement of their agenda.

Thanks to Trump, immigration is at the heart of the 2016 election. What has Obama done for the country's 54 million Latinos? The DREAM Act – DREAM is an acronym standing for Development, Relief, and Education for Alien Minors – had been kicking around Washington D.C. since 2001. It had sought to provide conditions of residency for those who had long been in the country, contributing peacefully to American life. Bush's attempts at comprehensive immigration reform had been scotched when hard-line conservatives had rejected – as they still do – the idea of a path to citizenship for undocumented immigrants. The Democrats picked up a version of it up in 2009, but in late 2010, the bill suffered a series of defeats. On this occasion, Republicans – still in Obama sabotage mode – raised issues of enforcement as a deal-breaker, thus providing the electorate with the depressing spectacle of a practical issue trumping a moral urgency. It is often stated that deportations were higher than ever before in the first years of the Obama administration, and while that is true, it should be remembered that attempts to tackle the issue legislatively were afoot and appeared to have bipartisan support. Had Obama moved to executive action early in his administration, it's possible those efforts might have been stymied. Of course, they were stymied in any case: the President had again underestimated the venom ranged against him. There is great justice in the *No Se Puede* ('No We Can't') posters which circulate on websites dedicated to Latino issues. Obama was labelled the deporter-in-chief: his administration has sponsored, inadvertently or not, the emergence of the quasi-Dickensian figure of the border agent, who is no longer content to patrol the borderline, but instead goes out into the cities, seeking people to deport.

Things were getting out of hand. Without some form of action, Obama would bequeath to his successor – as Bush bequeathed to him – little better than an airy intention and a record of cruelty. Obama turned to executive action. For some, there was opportunism involved: a general election was a year away, and the Latino vote would be crucial to winning the

Fig 8. In immigration reform, Obama did not meet expectations. His 2008 election slogan rebounded on him, with Yes, We Can becoming *No Se Puede* (No, We Can't).[60]

election, in particular the swing state of Florida. Yet there is no reason to believe Obama was unaffected by the hardship of deportation, particularly where children were involved. In June 2012, Obama introduced Deferred Action for Childhood Arrivals by executive order. It provides undocumented immigrants who entered the country before their 16th birthdays and before June 2007 with the chance to apply for a renewable two-year work permit and exemption from deportation. This wasn't the kind of sweeping reform the DREAM Act would have provided, but it was something. Politically, it worked: in 2012, the Pew Research Center estimates that the Latino vote went 71% to 27% in favour of Obama. Obama expanded the measures in 2014, and they are now the subject of bitter litigation. But unfair deportations still continue and House Speaker Paul Ryan has depressingly stated that immigration reform would go no further in 2016 – a reversal of his previous insistence that he would work to provide a path to citizenship.

Climate change was always going to be a tough sell: it asked the electorate to look both forward in time and also beyond its own borders to consider the wider health of the planet. Even so, there is evidence that the administration missed the chance to bring its cap-and-trade bill, The American Clean Energy and Security Act, to the Senate simply because they didn't sell it right. The administration had seen polls which suggested it would be better to sell cap-and-trade to the American people in terms of the green jobs it would create, not in terms of the science which pointed to climate change as an existential threat. Lee Wasserman, director of the Rockefeller Family Fund, was withering:

Had Lyndon Johnson likewise relied on polling, he would have told the Rev. Dr. Martin Luther King Jr. to talk only about the expanded industry and jobs that Southerners would realize after passage of a federal civil rights act. I could imagine Dr. King's response.[61]

It was the pattern we're now familiar with. Again the administration sought a golden mean, and again it pleased few – except that on this occasion nothing passed. Liberals were disappointed by a watered-down bill. They were particularly incensed that the coal and oil companies had enjoyed a seat at the negotiating table. Republicans had never been expected to support it in any case. When it failed, Obama turned in this instance also to unilateral action. The Clean Power Plan announced in August 2015 ambitiously aims to reduce carbon emissions by 32 per cent from 2005 levels by 2030.[62] Grunwald is among those impressed by the scope and proactiveness of the Obama administration here:

> I was aware that Obama was doubling fuel-efficiency standards for cars, and

I even knew he was pushing a flurry of lower-profile efficiency mandates for appliances. But I had no clue that just one of those rules, for commercial air conditioners, will singlehandedly reduce US energy use by 1 %.[63]

Meanwhile, the bid of Canadian energy company TransCanada to build the Keystone XL pipeline was rejected not so much because of any significant rise in carbon emissions it was expected to bring, but because of the perception that a go-ahead would have created: it was a way of drawing attention to the seriousness of the crisis in the lead-up to global climate-change negotiations in Paris in 2015. Killing the pipeline leant the administration credibility on the international stage at a crucial moment. Likewise, progress made internationally began to chip away at Obama's critics' reputation at home: in his 2016 State of the Union, Obama was able to point out that the Republican Party was alone in refusing to accept the science behind climate change. International progress has also been notable: Obama achieved a bilateral agreement with China, where the latter committed to lowering its carbon emissions by 2030, and to increasing its use of wind and solar power to 20% by the same year. Nor was the Keystone pipeline killed for nothing: the administration was also instrumental in securing an agreement with 196 countries in Paris, the first time the world had come together to address the problem. This agreement – much fêted but not legally binding – states that all countries, developed and developing, are to limit their emissions to 2C, will commit to aspire to lower them further to 1.5C, and will submit to regular reviews. Finance will be provided to poorer nations, and urgent aid delivered to any nation affected by climate-related disaster. It is another clear instance of Obama's proceeding on the basis of an Enlightenment understanding of the world, and of the Republicans resolutely opposing that view.

On both immigration and climate change, Obama made progress. But it is progress which is extremely easy to undo. Legislation is difficult to reverse – especially if it proves popular with the electorate. An executive order can be cancelled with the swish of a presidential pen. How durable the change will prove is entirely dependent on who succeeds Obama. But the scientific consensus is that to revert to anything

like the Bush approach would be – quite literally
– catastrophic.

THE WORLD STAGE

Presidents face regular interruptions; it is
a job beset by contingencies. Domestically,
Obama has faced surprise storms, regular gun
attacks, and the BP Oil spillage. Abroad, he has
sometimes appeared to look on helplessly at
the emergence of ISIS in the Middle East and at
events in Libya and Syria. But arguably his single
biggest foreign policy decision was well within
his own control. It was announced in a televised
address from the Oval Office on August 31st,
2010:

> The American combat mission in Iraq
> has ended. Operation Iraqi Freedom is
> over, and the Iraqi people now have lead
> responsibility for the security of their
> country.[64]

This statement was technically true, but it gave
a false impression. 50,000 troops remained
behind in an advisory capacity so that although
Operation Iraqi Freedom had ended, and

Operation New Dawn had begun, there was natural crossover between the two: both entailed a presence of troops in Iraq. Still, it was an important move, and one doesn't envy Obama's having to make the decision: the President has been forced throughout to weigh his initial campaign promise of withdrawal from foreign wars against the potential humanitarian cost of doing so. Coverage today, which tends to focus on the continuation of air strikes in Iraq, can sometimes fail to emphasise the extent of the shift that has occurred under Obama's presidency. Obama would attempt to explain this in his 2016 State of the Union address:

> We also can't try to take over and rebuild every country that falls into crisis. That's not leadership; that's a recipe for quagmire, spilling American blood and treasure that ultimately weakens us. It's the lesson of Vietnam, of Iraq—and we should have learned it by now.[65]

Obama's failings in this area usually have their roots in Bush-era policies. Obama is guilty perhaps of messy withdrawal, but the initial war was not his.

Should we be surprised that Obama has a patchy record on foreign policy? The world is never less than chaotic, and so it must be said that all presidents do as well, if every civil war and uprising worldwide is held to redound to them. Nevertheless, in his debit column would certainly be his assessment that American troops had left behind a 'sovereign, stable and self-reliant'[66] Iraq. The group of radical militants called ISIS emerged to upend this notion, spreading with astonishing brutality throughout Iraq and over an insubstantial border into Syria. With respect to ISIS, many now argue that Obama, naturally disinclined to warfare, has been slow to act when a just war has come along: he is the victim of his predecessor having cried wolf. Once again, his middle position has proven unpopular: he is also accused of being trigger-happy with drone strikes in Pakistan. Around 2,464 militants have been killed by drones, and most of those at Obama's orders, but he is also responsible for the deaths of at least 314 civilians.[67] Like so many presidents and prime ministers before him, Obama has weighed things in the balance and found that a strategy involving the collateral murder of women and children seems to be his least bad option.

In Iraq, the arrival of ISIS further hampered the emergence of a viable state. In Syria, the effects were even worse: the toxicity of Islamic fundamentalism rushed into an already-complex civil war, and added further misery to a country that had seemed to have reached the height of woe. Obama wavered on precisely what President Assad's use of chemical weapons against his citizens would mean. The images of the sarin-caused deaths appeared to argue for the moral imperative of air strikes: Secretary of State John Kerry was especially in favour. There was initial talk of a red line having been crossed. The President would later change his mind on the issue, and would tell Jeffrey Goldberg of *The Atlantic* that he was 'very proud of'[68] the decision not to go in. Such language can look somewhat odd next to the testimony of, for example, Lubna al-Kanawati, a worker in a Syrian refugee center:

> After Obama's failure to act over sarin, a profound sense of depression and isolation afflicted the people. They knew they'd die hungry and in silence, ignored by the world.[69]

Syria today is hell on earth: it is one of the most complicated battlefields the world has ever seen, and is a depressing example of how a movement undertaken in hope and freedom can come to nothing if it fails to cohere geographically and if it meets stubborn opposition from those whose interests do not align with it. It has also in itself contributed to a refugee crisis in Europe; this has, in turn, threatened the stability of the European Union, as we glimpsed in the prologue. The nobility of following through on a campaign promise of withdrawal from Iraq doesn't always seem to have been worth it when set against the carnage and uncertainty that followed.

Fig 9. Azaz, Syria in 2012. In this instance, Obama chose not to intervene.[70]

Fig 10. Obama with Raul Castro in Cuba, 2016.[71]

However, a few things must be said in
mitigation. The first is that President Assad
– and Putin and the Iranians who have been
propping him up – must bear the brunt of the
blame. Evil done by others is not Obama's fault.
Second, the claims made by the 2016 Republican
candidates that Obama has somehow rendered
America weak are exploded by the fact that,
under a Republican president, neither the war
in Iraq nor its parent conflict in Afghanistan
had been won. Obama inherited the weakness
that always ensues from misguided policy. The
President has signalled repeatedly in interviews
that he might have been more persuaded by the
case for air strikes in Syria if the Iraq example

hadn't been so raw and fresh. Third, it isn't clear that attacks from the air would really have helped as much as those who would talk up the Free Syria Army have suggested. Obama has been much derided for referring to the freedom-fighters as merely 'farmers and dentists': it was an unfortunate description of an exceptionally brave people whose rise up against tyranny should have generated a more admiring response from the leader of the free world. But as we shall see in the case of Libya (see below), Obama is surely right to fear another quagmire in the Middle-East. For a long time the closest commentators could get to an Obama doctrine was the oft-repeated: 'Don't do stupid shit.' We might not always find this a wholly impressive foreign policy mantra but it must also be said that, by and large, he hasn't.

The intervention in Libya in 2011 is the closest Obama came to breaking his own rule. When uprisings occurred in Egypt against President Hosni Mubarak, the administration had been divided. Obama's heart lay with the protestors, and he eventually urged Mubarak to go. An appetite for self-rule flared up across the northern coast of Africa. The wonderfully-named Jasmine Revolution in Tunisia saw the ouster of

the corrupt president Zine El Abidine Ben Ali.
But when the people of Libya rose up, beginning
with protests in 2009, they were taking on an
especially ruthless dictator, even by the harsh
standards of the region, in the shape of Colonel
Gaddafi.

While Obama was on a trip in South
America, it emerged that Gaddafi was
marching on Benghazi and set to slaughter
the population there – as Gaddafi put it, 'like
rats'. These circumstances are a useful insight
into the Obama foreign policy: wishing to turn
his attention to other continents, the Middle-
East always comes calling. As Gaddafi neared
Benghazi, the French President Nicolas Sarkozy
let it be known he was keen for an invasion, as
did UK Prime Minister David Cameron. Obama
agreed. The Benghazi slaughter was averted,
but the situation today is, in the words of Obama
himself, a 'shit show' with no serious hope of
stable government emerging anytime soon.[72]
However, the invasion hasn't set off the same
fury that the Iraq invasion did for a number
of reasons: it was triggered by an immediate
humanitarian crisis; there was genuine multi-
lateral support, enshrined in UN resolution
1973; the reasoning behind the decision to go

in was open and there was no equivalent of the contortions over WMD that we have already seen in relation to the Iraq invasion; ground troops were not committed; and there has been an honest post-war admission of failures from the President himself, which could hardly be more at odds with the post-Iraq dodging and weaving of, for example, Tony Blair.

Obama plainly considers dealing with the Middle-East one of the least enjoyable parts of his job: he is far happier at a Latin American or pan-Asian summit, where he knows that the countries he is dealing with are on an upward curve. The fruit of this – not a pleasant fruit for some – is the Trans-Pacific Partnership signed on February 4th 2016 between 12 Pacific Rim countries including Australia, Japan, and Canada. If ratified, it would be the largest trade deal in history.

Is there an Obama Doctrine? The President will often frame his foreign policy decisions in relation to those which Reagan faced. The Soviet Union, he argues, was an existential threat to the US and to the Western way of life, in a way that Islamic fundamentalism and countries such as Iran, Cuba and even Putin's comparatively weak Russia are not.

There is truth to this: ISIS's army is estimated at about 30,000. At the time of its fall, the Soviet Union numbered over 280 million. The brutality of ISIS's crimes sometimes gives an impression of greater importance than it has. In the years 2001 to 2013, 406,496 people died by firearms on US soil. In the same years, 350 citizens were killed overseas by acts of terrorism – 3,380 if you include the September 11th attacks on American soil.[73] So when Obama speaks of ISIS, as he did in a press conference in Malaysia after the Paris attacks, as 'a bunch of killers with good social media', it is a deliberate attempt at proportion: to panic is to write ISIS's recruitment materials for them. He cannot in any case be called soft on terrorism: Al-Qaeda has been decimated under Obama. He must also be given credit for orchestrating the crafty mission which led to the death of Osama bin Laden in May of 2011: were bin Laden still alive, we would certainly be hearing from Donald Trump about the travesty of Obama's failure to kill him.

His policy of reopening relations with Cuba, and his nuclear agreement with Iran, where sanctions were lifted in exchange for a 98% reduction in Iran's nuclear program, are of a piece with these policies. Obama views both countries as threats far different in scale from the fascist and communist threats of the 20th century, and so claims a licence to try diplomatic solutions. In relation to Cuba, it already looks like a sensible correction to an outdated policy. His visit in 2016 may have contained some uncomfortable moments, but they all belonged to Raul Castro. The Iran nuclear agreement is far harder to second-guess. There can be little doubt that Iran's theocratic regime is a powerful influence for destabilisation in the Middle-East, funding Hezbollah, Shiite rebels in Yemen, and of course Assad. Iran is now wealthier than it was, and Obama is betting a lot on the next generation, and on the next president. There remains the possibility that he is seeing the Iran he wants to see. However, attempting to defuse the Middle East still looks smarter than bombing it, as many in the Republican Party, from John McCain to Ted Cruz, have fantasised about doing.

WHAT WAS LEFT UNDONE

This has been a brief tour through a largely enlightened – indeed largely Enlightenment – presidency.

The Obama administration has engaged sincerely with the facts of the world. It has instituted some messy but important reforms. A more tolerant society has emerged: Obama became the first sitting president to visit a federal prison, he was the first to endorse gay marriage, was the first to appoint a transgender White House staff member, and recently made a pointed visit to a Baltimore mosque in the aftermath of Donald Trump's calls for a shutdown on Muslims entering the country. He has delivered some important orations such as his 'Amazing Grace' speech in Charleston at the funeral of the senselessly gunned-down Reverend Clementa C. Pinckney, and his speech in Selma on the 60th anniversary of the civil rights marches. He has vividly expressed his frustration with the gun lobby. He has also conducted himself with undeniable grace and good humour in the face of attacks which have often had a rancidly racist tinge. All these things, relatively limited in policy terms, have added to the tone of his administration and may in aggregate be counted important in themselves.

Yet all governments have sequels and dangling threads. By the fourth quarter of the

Obama presidency, it was becoming clear what the outstanding issues would be. On the foreign policy side, the Iran deal will need oversight. A resolution to the Syrian conflict and the defeat of ISIS are certain to be outstanding, perhaps even for the president after this next one. On the domestic front, comprehensive immigration reform still hasn't been passed. The economy has recovered, though it is hardly booming, and vulnerable to cross-currents from China. The Paris climate change agreement needs to be strengthened to better handle the severity of the problem.

It has also become clear that the next president will need to address the issue of economic inequality, which has increased under Obama. The top 1% took home 18.12% of income in 2009. In 2012, that had risen to 22.46%. In 2013, economist Angus Deaton wrote:

> There is a danger that the rapid growth of top incomes can become self-reinforcing through the political access that money can bring. Rules are set not in the public interest but in the interest of the rich, who use those rules to become yet richer and more influential.[74]

This was still substantially true by the time the campaigns began to kick-off. In fact those words, from the pen of a Nobel Prize-winning economist, sound like a promo for the Bernie Sanders campaign. Obama has done more than one might think to reverse this rampant growth in inequality. In May 2016, his administration released new rules on overtime pay which will improve the lot of some 12.5 million workers. In addition, Obamacare is an essentially redistributionist policy which provides aid and subsidies to lower income workers paid for out of higher taxes for the rich. Even so, in both the Democratic and the Republican primaries, as we shall see, wages – and in particular their relationship to international trade – would be defining issues as the campaign season went into full swing.

And so on to the 2016 election. On the face of it, the country looked reasonably well-off. True, there had been bitter feuds, but there had been bitter feuds up until 2012, and that election had turned out to be a more or less run-of-the-mill affair between the incumbent and a predictable Republican candidate, Mitt Romney. By 2016, unemployment had dipped; people were signing up for Obamacare. The auto industry was thriving. Wars had been wound down. Yes, new ones had arisen in their stead, but America had at least been smart enough not to get too deeply embroiled in them this time around. It had led the way in the fight against climate change. As Jeb Bush, brother of George W. Bush, watched the donations roll into his coffers, and as a rested Hillary Clinton prepared again for a gruelling run for the presidency, the presumption was that this would be business-as-usual: an election in fact between two familiar political dynasties.

But somewhere in the eight years of the Obama administration, something had snapped. The accumulated rancour, the images of beheadings in the deserts, stagnant wages, and the sense that this was not how America should be all went into the pot. The media gave it a big stir. A chemical reaction was about to happen.

It is now time to write words whose seismic impact not even the protagonist himself foresaw: Enter Donald Trump.

PART III

THE REPUBLICANS
IN 2016

CHAPTER 5 – ENTER DONALD TRUMP

Half of the American people have never read a newspaper. Half never voted for President. One hopes it is the same half.

– Gore Vidal

Occasionally in politics a chancer enters the fray, and almost to their own surprise, takes hold. The signature Donald Trump shrug at one of his surrealist rallies during the early part of 2016, as he recited his poll numbers, suggested a certain surprise about what was happening that bluster couldn't quite hide. Did Trump expect all this? Obama appears to have thought not, baiting the press at the 2016 White House Correspondents' Dinner:

> Because I think we can all agree that from the start, he's gotten the appropriate amount of coverage, befitting the seriousness of his candidacy. (Laughter and applause.)

> I hope you all are proud of yourselves. (Laughter.) The guy wanted to give his

hotel business a boost, and now we're praying that Cleveland makes it through July.[75]

But it was probably more than publicity. Trump is both self-confident, and profoundly competitive: he is not the kind of man to enter things he doesn't believe he can win. One of his favourite insults is 'loser'.

Of course politics has always been – at least in part – an elaborate game of dice. All prime ministers and presidents seize a certain moment, and are plucked from the ranks of also-rans into a limelight whose brightness must addle them. Even the most seemingly principled or monomaniacal tend to adjust their positions: the great historian Alan Bullock considered Adolf Hitler primarily an opportunist. In the UK, David Cameron and George Osborne, those supposed ideologues, have both performed notable U-turns in the last few months alone.

But if Donald Trump is an opportunist, he is also one who has carefully stacked the odds in his own favour: he is a billionaire adventurer who can afford to do what he likes, even lose. The flipside of his love of, as he tends to put it, 'winning, winning, winning,' is that he pays almost no attention to setbacks. His defeat in the first contest in Iowa in January 2016 appeared only to reinforce his sense of himself, and triggered no self-doubt: it simply became the greatest second-place finish ever. He may be the first to perfect shamelessness at the level of presidential politics. Nixon might have been cavalier enough to embark on the events that led to Watergate, but he spent the rest of his life trying to 'rebuild' his image. Under similar circumstances, one suspects Trump wouldn't bother. Tony Blair still hasn't apologised for the Iraq War, but the adamance of his refusal – the strangled denial, the lined face – is a function of embarrassment. Trump inhabits a world of comparative bliss: apology is simply not his style.

This imperviousness has been purchased. His candidacy plays on his wealth – it is the singular thing about him. He is not entirely anomalous in this regard: Ross Perot leveraged his personal fortune to run as a candidate in 1992, and in early 2016, Michael Bloomberg was reportedly considering a run for the presidency as an independent candidate. Failed presidential candidates Mitt Romney and John Kerry also had fortunes around the $200 million mark. But in these last two instances, each candidate exhibited subservience to their respective political machines. Trump, who might have run as an independent like Perot, represents something new in that he is leveraging his own wealth in an attempt to commandeer an existing party structure for his own ends. The closest thing to Trump in modern day politics is Italy's Silvio Berlusconi – in Berlusconi there is the same fortune made in construction and media, the same cheerful hedonism darkened by casual racism, and a similar defiance of criticism. Rambling solipsism and a freewheeling thin skin complete the picture.

It is hard to find precursors in American life. His surrealist style is reminiscent of Sarah Palin. He also shares with Palin – and increasingly, with the party he has been able to commandeer – a highly contemptuous attitude toward facts. In hailing from the world of light entertainment, he can – and does – point to Reagan as a precursor.

The Trump phenomenon didn't come from nowhere, but it is undeniably a piece of cutting-edge political kitsch. The US wasn't quite ready for this in 2012, but it is apparently ready for it now.

THE EARLY LIFE OF THE DONALD

Born in 1946, Donald John Trump had advantages in life. His father, Fred, was a real estate developer. Young Donald was assiduously cordoned off from the diversity of America, growing up in a mock Tudor revival home on the Jamaica Estates in Queens, New York. As a boy, Donald was not easy: the same man who would later look on with some approval when a Black Lives Matter activist was beaten up at one of his rallies, and even offer to pay the legal fees of the assailant, was 'a pretty rough fellow when he was small', according to his father who, noting this trait, enrolled Donald at the New York Military Academy.

Donald moved from there to Fordham University and then on to Wharton Business School. There is an intriguing biographical black hole in his subsequent non-involvement in the Vietnam War: Trump was eligible for the draft upon leaving Wharton but drew a high number after receiving a medical deferment, possibly on account of heel spurs. One thread of his career is his outspoken concern for the welfare of veterans – in February 2016 he skipped a *Fox News* debate ostensibly to raise money for them – but he avoided military service himself.

Fred loaned Donald his first million, and from that moment on Trump's life can be told mainly in deals. He longed for more than his father's life of developing middle class housing. By 1971 he had moved to Manhattan and was already engaged on large building projects. He came excitingly close to disaster when the acquisition of the Taj Mahal Casino led to mounting debt and a declaration of bankruptcy: Trump was fortunate that banks and bondholders opted to restructure the debt. It was the only time he was in serious danger of personal bankruptcy. From that moment on he had many business successes: the world has been surprisingly tolerant about his desire to place ugly buildings on its skyline, and to fill those buildings with kitsch memorabilia. Most businessmen are content with anonymity: Trump craved both money *and* attention. The distinguishing characteristic of his career is narcissism. The deals piled up and, in time, Donald joined the ranks of the superrich. He doesn't always compare favourably with his contemporaries among that small group: next to the activism of Bill Gates or Warren Buffet, his charitable work appears negligible – in fact, it is as close to nothing as a billionaire could reasonably get away with. There are records of donations here and there to the American Cancer Society, American Diabetes Association, Alliance for Lupus Research, Autism Speaks, and the Crohn's & Colitis Foundation of America, among others. But Trump's main energies have plainly been devoted to expansion of the Trump brand. His business practices are almost always exploitative and rarely, if ever, contributive.

The world has been given a startling number of things with Trump's name on them. There is Trump Mortgage, Trump Restaurants, Trump Buffets, Trump Chocolate, Trump Ice and Trump Steaks. The public has sometimes expressed a limited appetite for these products. Many franchises have been discontinued among them the doomed Trump Vodka (2005-2011, and launched under the banner 'Success distilled'), *Trump Magazine* (2007-2009) and Trump: The Game (started in 1989, relaunched in 2005, now discontinued). Trump's career teaches us that billionaires can try many things and see what happens: his presidential run should be seen in this context.

An interest in the arts does not feature in Donald Trump's life. In 1980, he authorised the destruction of a pair of 15-foot-high bas-relief sculptures on the Bonwit-Teller building in New York, though the sculptures had been promised to the Metropolitan Museum of Art.[76] He famously stated that his second favourite book, after the Bible, was his own *The Art of the Deal*. His music taste is popular, but he talks about it in terms of who he knows rather than any particular appreciation for the music ('Aerosmith is terrific...they're big fans of mine', 'Jon Bon Jovi is a great guy', 'Michael Jackson lived in my building'[77]). Popular musicians are part of his world. As we shall see, Donald Trump has been called a fascist. If so, he exhibits nothing resembling Hitler's love of Wagner, or his minor talent as an artist. This isn't in itself consoling, since it is very possible to imagine fascist-style radicalism carried out by someone with a different taste in music than Hitler's. Ian Kershaw once pointed out that Hitler read in order to confirm his own prejudices: the suggestion is that the prejudice was there before the reading was. Trump's authoritarianism partakes of the vacuity of the age. He at least gets points for honesty on this score: 'I've been focused on jobs, money and deals, that's what I do.'[78]

There is dispute as to his wealth. Estimates vary wildly, from Timothy L. O'Brien's provocative figure of $150 million,[79] to *Forbes*' thorough estimation of $4.1 billion.[80] Trump estimates his own wealth at $8,737,540,000,[81] and according to *Forbes*, 'consistently pushes for a higher net worth — especially when it comes to the value of his personal brand'.[82] A high net worth is important for a business which is based on loaning his name. It is also vital for his presidential campaign, which is centred on the idea that he is one of life's winners, and that this ability to win will, in the event of victory, be osmotically bequeathed by a President Trump to the nation at large.

TRUMP'S ANNOUNCEMENT

The Republican Party is in fact the only entity that Donald Trump has been associated with for any length of time which he hasn't yet been able to name after himself. There is little doubt however that, after having won the nomination, he intends to remake the G.O.P. in his own image, and there is still the possibility, though remoter with every passing day, that the party will split as a result. The gumption of it all was clear from the off. Trump announced his candidacy on June 16th 2015 in – where else? – Trump Tower in New York, with the claim that he would 'make America great again' (Fig 11). He sounded straightaway the main note on his lyre: immigration.

> The US has become a dumping ground for everybody else's problems. [Applause] Thank you. It's true, and these are the best and the finest. When Mexico sends its people, they're not sending their best. They're not sending you. They're not sending you. They're sending people that have lots of problems, and they're bringing those problems with us. They're bringing drugs. They're bringing crime. They're rapists. And some, I assume, are good people.

This statement shows the Trump method. It is a riff – a kind of bigoted jazz. It evokes a general anger: the language only needs to skim off one specific – in this case Mexico – to provide it with context, but really all the speech needs is the implications of its tone: things are not as they should be. It could be easily recast – and in the general election no doubt will be – endlessly upon different themes. Trump's language is reliably emotive: among the usual suits and soundbite-purveyors of the modern political primary, he can resemble a barbarian at a Regency tea party. His dizzying unscriptedness appeals to voters, who see it as the antidote to the dire, autocued speeches of professional pols. The style also frees him from the obligation to be factual. The words 'I assume' show that external factual reality matters less to him than his own opinion – in that sense, it's the speech of a wealthy man used to being listened to by subordinates. If challenged over data, he tends to express impatience and often refers in shadowy terms to 'lots of articles' which back up his opinion.

Fig 11. Donald Trump in Trump Tower where he made his June 16th 2015 announcement. In relation to Mexicans he said: 'They're bringing drugs. They're bringing crime. They're rapists. And some, I assume, are good people'.[83]

Particularly on the Democrat side, you tend to find the speakers, whether Obama or Clinton or Sanders, operating very differently. They will cite data, express worry at the human cost behind that data, and suggest a way to improve things. Here, for instance, is Obama in January 2016 suggesting changes to solitary confinement in the US:

> There are as many as 100,000 people held in solitary confinement in US prisons — including juveniles and people with mental illnesses. As many as 25,000 inmates are serving months, even years of their sentences alone in a tiny cell, with almost no human contact...It has been linked to depression, alienation, withdrawal, a reduced ability to interact with others and the potential for violent behaviour...The Justice Department has completed its review, and I am adopting its recommendations to reform the federal prison system. These include banning solitary confinement for juveniles and as a response to low-level infractions, expanding treatment for the mentally ill and increasing the amount

of time inmates in solitary can spend outside of their cells.[84]

The above is from a newspaper article, but any number of speeches would showcase the same rhetorical method. A problem is flagged; evidence is stated; solutions based on that evidence are put forward. By contrast, Trump works himself into a rage but he is usually offering nothing but rage itself.

AFTER THE ANNOUNCEMENT

Most in the Republican Party and in the media listened to the Trump announcement and assumed that his candidacy would never amount to anything. Once the media found out that Trump helped ratings, they began giving Trump enormous amounts of air time – effectively free publicity. By mid-March in 2016, the firm mediaQuant put a value on the free coverage. Establishment favourite Jeb Bush had spent $82 million in paid media – television ads – and received $214 million in free media generated by network coverage. Trump, by contrast, had spent a mere $10 million in paid media, and received $1.9 billion for free from the networks.

This amount was unprecedented, and a sure sign that greed is alive and well in the corridors of television studios. In February, CBS head Les Moonves had been surprisingly open on the topic, and entered the cast of this election's villains at the same time: 'The money's rolling in and this is fun.... (the) Trump phenomenon may not be good for America but it's damned good for CBS'.[85]

There was also a hubristic side to this: most assumed that Trump couldn't win because he was so obviously ill-suited to the job. His policy platform was thin, and remains so: surely so unsuitable an applicant could not prevail. This still looked like the case in January, when a second-place finish in Iowa to Ted Cruz seemed to create the possibility that his campaign would flame out dramatically. Right into late April, there would be an air of denial about the Republican Party and the media. The world, arguably, at time of writing, is still in denial.

One can sympathise with them. The mystery still percolates today: 'Why does Donald Trump play to voters at all?' None of the available answers feels wholly satisfactory: or rather the likely causes have had effects out of all proportion to what they merit. The fact is that his inflammatory rhetoric matched certain fears, particularly among low-educated blue-collar workers, which we have already glimpsed arising during the Obama era. Obama's withdrawal from Iraq and his drawdown of troops in Afghanistan, were seen by some voters not as a wise recalibration after a series of rash mistakes, but as a defeatist admission: America is not as powerful as all that. Images on the news of hooded ISIS fighters set to behead American captive James Foley reinforced a sense of unease and alarm. Tragic as the death of Foley was, in an image-driven culture, a solitary event can have power beyond its actual import. In addition, the Great Recession had created the stagnation in wages that we have already glanced at: the need to blame someone created a certain receptivity to Trump's anti-immigration message. Further still, the peculiar character of these problems may have contributed; each has an intractable and entrenched feel. When the mind is baffled, emotion rushes in. Ryan Lizza of *The New Yorker* reported from an early Trump rally:

> Trump's fans tend to express little regard for political norms. They cheer at his most outlandish statements. [Fox New

presenter] O'Reilly asked Trump if he meant it when he said that he would "take out" the family members of terrorists. He didn't believe that Trump would "put out hits on women and children" if he were elected. Trump replied, "I would do pretty severe stuff." The Mesa crowd erupted in applause. "Yeah, baby!" a man near me yelled. I had never previously been to a political event at which people cheered for the murder of women and children.[86]

The sense that Trump might just do the unthinkable creates a sense of possibility, of new parameters. It is wholly an illusion, but it appears to be appealing if you happen to be angry.

Another reason for Trump's success was that America has never loved conventional politicians. In Reagan it elected an actor, and in Clinton Americans had seen a cool guy who played saxophone on *The Arsenio Hall Show*. By contrast, in the second half of the 20th century, the more strait-laced characters – Gerald Ford, George H.W. Bush and Jimmy Carter – have earned the rebuke of one-term presidencies. The trend continued into the 2000s. The electorate preferred the folksy and affable George Bush to both the technocrat Al Gore and the dry John Kerry. In Obama, they had sought to elect a transformational figure, someone 'outside the Washington beltway'.

In a climate of 24-hour news, Americans also tend to tire of their current president and are likely to elect someone with the opposite traits of the incumbent. As David Axelrod, former chief strategist to Obama, has written: 'So who among the Republicans is more the antithesis of Mr. Obama than the trash-talking, authoritarian, give-no-quarter Mr. Trump?'[87]

Obama's presence in the White House feeds Trump's main message: the first black president is a ready symbol for the bogus contention that illegal immigrants are taking jobs from 'true' Americans. Trump joins the UK's Nigel Farage and France's Marie Le Pen among those who have successfully given vent to fears about the porosity of borders. Like them, Trump does so in defiance of his country's centre-right – the difference is that Trump does so not by founding a far right party of his own, but while attempting to overrun an existing party apparatus. That in itself is vaguely thrilling because the party has behaved so childishly throughout the Obama years: he is a wrecking-ball swinging against loathed architecture.

Trump's appeal is especially galling to party elders since Trump is flying in the face of what they had expected to be standing for at this point in time: the Trump ascendancy is, one would have thought, a further toxification of its 'brand'. The Republican 'establishment' (we shall look in detail at what this phrase means in the next chapter) had attributed Mitt Romney's 2012 defeat, not to the candidate's famous gaffe where he expressed his disapproval of the government-dependant '47%', but to the party's intransigence on immigration. In Marco Rubio, who would have been the country's first Latino president, and in Jeb Bush, who speaks Spanish and has a Mexican wife, the party had hoped by 2016 to be appealing to a burgeoning Latino demographic. In defying inherited party wisdom, Trump's ascendancy is reminiscent of the rise of Jeremy Corbyn in the UK where the electorate took an obvious pleasure in disregarding the interventions of Tony Blair and Gordon Brown, as well as the expectations of the media. At times, the *National Review* crowd in the US has seemed as powerless in this election cycle as the New Labour aristocracy did in 2015.

And yet in other respects it isn't absolutely true to think of Trump only in terms of immigration. He isn't straightforward – his protean nature makes him hard to attack. Trump was a registered Democrat during the 1990s, and is on record as having favoured a version of healthcare reform which sounds remarkably similar to Obamacare. Even in this election he has said, in his dramatic way, that people shouldn't be dying in the streets, which suggests a commitment to the social safety net. He claims to champion Medicare, though on his current figures it is difficult to see how he could afford it (see below). He has admitted to giving money to the Clintons at various times. He favours protectionist economic policies. The protectionist impulse is usually in some sense a nostalgic one, and nostalgia cannot help but inhabit a less diverse world: the shoe – or perhaps one should say the glove – fits. Even so, protectionism isn't necessarily right wing – it is a position often favoured by the socialist left, and indeed Bernie Sanders and Donald Trump have broadly similar attitudes towards free trade in general and the Transatlantic Trade Partnership in particular.

Trump therefore makes one wonder just how ideologically right-wing a huge chunk of the so-called 'base' is – much to the embarrassment of the party who want it to be very right wing.

On the other hand, the far-right tone of some of his other policies – on immigration, his relaxed attitude to violence, and in his stated wish to bring back torture – makes one compelled to ask another question.

IS TRUMP A FASCIST?

In fact, commentators like Michael Tomasky of *The Daily Beast* prefer the term neo-Fascist, which feels about right. When George Orwell set *1984* in the UK, he was pointing out that fascism might occur anywhere and anytime: it was an encouragement towards vigilance.

The signs are worrying. Trump's attitude towards minorities is alarmingly reminiscent of that of previous fascist leaders. It is the kind of prejudice which makes one compelled to seek comparisons. Andrew Roberts has pointed out similarities between Mussolini and Trump: 'Mussolini – the other master of the ludicrously bombastic speech and the deliberately jutting jaw and the impossible-to-fulfil promises – is clearly Trump's secret template'.[88] Sometimes his strong-man grimace can look remarkably similar to that in old photos of Hitler attempting to project a similar strength. For most of the Republican primary, Trump's 'ceiling' was around 37%, roughly the same as Hitler's share of the vote in the lead-up to assuming the chancellorship in Germany.

Trump's trajectory over the course of the campaign is another cause for concern. During the early part of 2016, Trump's more fascist-resembling policies appeared to become more extreme over time. His call for a temporary ban on all Muslims entering the country in the wake of the Paris attacks went further than the remarks about Mexicans in his announcement speech. In justification, Trump points to FDR's worst decision, to detain Japanese nationals in the wake of Pearl Harbour: 'This was a president highly respected by all, he did the same thing'.[89] But in the Ryan Lizza excerpt I quoted a moment ago, Trump has also implied that 'the families of terrorists' could not expect clement treatment from him. In a famous essay 'Ur-Fascism' Umberto Eco called this 'fear of difference', and Trump exhibits such fear in high degree. This aspect of Trumpism also has its roots in the

Know Nothings of the 1840s, with their slogan, aimed at Irish Roman Catholic immigrants: 'Americans must rule America'.

Trump's prescription for the ills he perceives comes close to Eco's description of fascists as touting 'action for action's sake'. Jamelle Bouie continues in an excellent article for *Slate*:

> Trump promises action. He will cut new deals and make foreign competitors subordinate. He will deport immigrants and build a wall on the border, financed by Mexico. He will bring "spectacular" economic growth.[90]

To a false diagnosis, Trump prescribes a vague cure. The effect is that by the time adversaries start to challenge him, they are already two steps away from reality. When challenged, he is already on his own turf. Indeed the very attempt to challenge him only reinforces his weak versus strong narrative: he creates a dialogue in which to question him is to concede his relevance, and thereby to reinforce it. John Kasich, the moderate Ohio governor, was expressing this frustration when he said at the fourth

Republican debate in 2015 in relation to Trump's immigration ideas: 'It's a silly argument. It's not an adult argument. We all know you can't pick them up and ship them back across the border.' It was true, but it sounded plaintive.

Amid it all – and not mentioned in Eco's essay or in Bouie's *Slate* article – is something at least as important: it is Trump's lack of a sense of humour when the joke's on him which again recalls the dictators of the 20th century. Humour has always antagonised dictators. In recent history, one frequently finds 'serious' intellectuals (George Bernard Shaw and H.G. Wells are examples) slower to understand fascism for what it is than comedians like Charlie Chaplin or P.G. Wodehouse. Examples of Trump's clashing with comedians abound: for instance, he attempted an absurd lawsuit against comedic chat show host Bill Maher, after Maher offered to donate $5 million to the charity of Trump's choice if he could prove that he was not 'the spawn of his mother having sex with an orangutan'.[91] But here again Trumpism feels like a mutation of the fascist gene. His specific brand of telegenic buffoonery is difficult to compare with that of any other historical figure. For instance, in November of 2015, he had the wherewithal to go on *Saturday Night Live*, the nation's most important satirical programme. This was a rather grubby episode: it's hard not to feel that *SNL*'s decision to reverse its former ban on Donald Trump was ratings-driven. In doing so, the show's producers surely implied that it considered Trump's previous remarks towards Mexicans, the disabled, and Muslims as not that serious to begin with. The implication is that he deserved an opportunity to shrug them off. Trump began his monologue: 'A lot of greats have hosted this show including me in 2004... We're going to have a lot of fun tonight.'

Then, the comedian Larry David intervened, in what was meant to sound like a spontaneous heckle: 'You're a racist.'

Trump replied: 'Who the hell, I knew that was going to happen. Who is that?'

David repeated in a stilted way: 'Trump's a racist.'

Trump: 'It's Larry David. What are you doing, Larry?'

David: 'I heard that if I yelled that they'd give me $5,000.'

Trump: 'As a businessman I can fully appreciate that.'[92]

The $5,000 in question was promised by Latino activist group DeportRacism.com to anyone who could interrupt Trump during the show. Afterwards the organisation released a statement saying they would pay David the money. But the skit had a scripted feel. David's anger was clearly simulated; Trump's bafflement insincere. Furthermore not only does David apologise for saying something that everyone knows is true (Trump really has said racist things) but he tees up Trump to remind the electorate again of the supposed strength of his wealth. This wasn't the thrilling heckle that was reported in the media, but a *folie à deux*.

Trump, like Goebbels, knows how the media works – except that it's a different media now. Rory Bremner used to say that you can't out-George Bush George Bush. The same is true of Trump, and this confers on him a kind of power. Besides, there comes a point at which momentum has been reached and mockery loses force: Wodehouse's character Roderick Spode, a would-be dictator who is embarrassed that he designs women's clothing, reminds us that there were many at the time who thought Hitler ridiculous. *The Code of the Woosters* was published in 1938. A lot happened after that:

finding someone absurd doesn't always render them harmless.

Trump's inability to laugh at himself is closely allied with self-pity. Eco wrote of fascism: 'The followers must feel humiliated by the ostentatious wealth and force of their enemies.'[93] Trump's resentment is not aimed towards those of superior wealth: it was noticeable in January 2016 how relaxed he was about the notion of Michael Bloomberg, a man richer than him, entering the race. Instead, Trump frequently refers to being treated 'unfairly'. In January 2016, he pulled out of the last *Fox News* debate, chaired by Megan Kelly, after the channel issued the following press release:

> We learned from a secret back channel that the Ayatollah and Putin both intend to treat Donald Trump unfairly when they meet with him if he becomes president – a nefarious source tells us that Trump has his own secret plan to replace the Cabinet with his Twitter followers to see if he should even go to those meetings.[94]

Incensed, Trump pulled out of the evening. What was noticeable here was his willingness to rise to so obvious a bait. Self-pity in him leads to impulsiveness: surely a disastrous trait in a potential president. The curious thing is that Trump has time again been rescued from corporate bankruptcy by what now seems a kind of excessive fairness: it is not quite clear where this rampaging sense of injustice has come from, except to say that radical narcissists are always experiencing a gulf between their own self-perception and the treatment accorded them in the world of real things.

For all this, there is still some doubt as to whether Trump really merits the term 'fascist'. He still hasn't put down the kind of 'on-the-ground' structures usually required for political extremist projects. Other fascists have built painstaking party apparatuses. Trump's narcissism may have led to organisational negligence: if he were to lose in November, what would be left of his campaign? Image politicians tend to have limited legacies: the apparent demise of New Labour in Britain shows how swiftly a movement built too much around a single figure can unravel. On the other hand, a defeated Trump would have enough money to run again in 2020, should he so wish. He would be 73 by then, but it is hard to imagine him not seeking revenge. The Trump-as-fascist argument is open to other objections. Fascism has tended to be closely aligned with dreams of international warfare. In so global a world, Trump's dreams don't particularly tend that way – probably he has already fulfilled most of them through his company. It has also been pointed out by John Cassidy in *The New Yorker* that Trump has so far cooperated with, indeed appeared to revel in, the democratic process. There is limited consolation to be had here: the US presidential elections with their dizzying expenditure, reality game-show debates, and limited focus on issues have suited his needs, and while he hasn't changed their structure, he has successfully changed their tenor. It is not hard to imagine him radically altering the presidency in the event he were elected. He has already refused to attend that debate, and this during the relatively hampered period when he is trying to get elected.

WHAT KIND OF PRESIDENT WOULD TRUMP BE?

It is difficult to predict how the presidency might act upon such a volatile personality. He is beholden to no one and so, more than most presidents, might be inclined to take risks: presidential tantrums would be a regular reality.

Trump would not be elected on any detailed policy platform: there would be little or nothing for him to be judged against. For most of the campaign, there were only five policy tabs on his campaign website – a sixth was added on healthcare reform in March. It is hard to think of someone ever running for high office on such a slender programme. His numbers are cavalier and do not add up. On the economy, he has pledged across-the-board tax cuts: the tax policy center finds that he would increase standard deduction amounts by around four times the current levels. Federal revenues would be decreased by $9.5 billion, which makes his claims that he would 'end Obamacare and replace it with something terrific, for far less money' hollow indeed. On his figures, other cuts would have to be made, perhaps in social security, though one can but guess. On immigration he would 'build a wall' and somehow – again he doesn't say how – make Mexico pay for it. There would be, surely, a huge increase in deportations, and Obama's executive actions in that area would certainly be rolled back.

On foreign policy, Trump has vowed to 'bring China to the negotiating table' and to renegotiate trade. This risks damaging the US's $120 billion of exports to that country: most likely, if Trump were to place a tariff on Chinese exports, China would simply retaliate and do likewise. But his administration would be broadly protectionist – the Trans-Pacific Trade Partnership would be scrapped. The Iran nuclear treaty would also become a 'tougher deal' – he hasn't yet said how or on what basis he would restructure it. Torture would once again occur in Guantanamo Bay, although it isn't clear from some testimony within the military that they would follow orders this time. Trump has stated without citing any science, that climate change is 'a total hoax', so we can assume the Paris Treaty would also be killed and Obama's EPA regulations rolled back. Fracking would thrive; the world would likely miss its window on climate change. Under Trump, any kind of gun control legislation would remain undone, although that will probably be the case no matter who is President.

The only certainty is that it would be an anti-Enlightenment administration. President

Obama recently explained to Glenn Thrush of *Politico*:

> 'You think about it: When I ran against John McCain, John McCain and I had real differences, sharp differences, but John McCain didn't deny climate science,' he said. 'John McCain didn't call for banning Muslims from the United States...[The] Republican vision has moved not just to the right, but has moved to a place that is unrecognizable.[95]

But there is one other particular in which the rise of Trump reminds one of fascism generally and of the circumstances of Hitler's elevation specifically. It is in the willingness of some powerful elements in America, weary and lacking in ideas, to accommodate him.

It is not uncommon to hear the question: 'How did this happen?'

The answer can only be found in the present state of the Republican Establishment. To understand the state of the party, one must delve into the early months of 2016. In the ordinary scheme of things, these primaries, so noisy while they are going on, tend to be forgotten with a sigh of relief once the party has united around its leader.

This time around, it's a live issue – even as I write, conservative grandees are calling for an alternative to Trump, and talk of a third-party run by the so-called #NeverTrump candidate shall probably persist at least so long as filing deadlines remain open – in most states, those deadlines close around 60 days before the November election. The Speaker of the House Paul Ryan initially stated that he couldn't contemplate supporting Trump. Neither George H.W. Bush nor George W. Bush are prepared to endorse him. When we wonder who will win in 2016, the answer will in part depend on how many traditional Republican voters go over to Hillary Clinton and how many stick with Trump. In order to begin to guess at this, it is important to know what apparatus he has commandeered, and how he managed it. And what went wrong for that shadowy entity the Republican establishment?

Actually at least three things went wrong: Donald Trump we know. The others were Ted Cruz and Jeb Bush.

CHAPTER 6 – THE REPUBLICAN ESTABLISHMENT

It appears, then, that the Eatanswill people, like the people of many other small towns, considered themselves of the utmost and most mighty importance, and that every man in Eatanswill, conscious of the weight that attached to his example, felt himself bound to unite, heart and soul, with one of the two great parties that divided the town – the Blues and the Buffs. Now the Blues lost no opportunity of opposing the Buffs, and the Buffs lost no opportunity of opposing the Blues; and the consequence was, that whenever the Buffs and Blues met together at public meeting, town-hall, fair, or market, disputes and high words arose between them.[96]

– Charles Dickens, *The Pickwick Papers*

When the results for the first contest in the Republican Party in the Iowa caucus came in on February 1st, 2016, there were several surprises in store. On the Republican side, victory went not to Donald Trump as polls had suggested but to Ted Cruz, an ideological conservative whose superior ground organisation and greater ability to connect with evangelicals saw him win 27.7% of the vote, edging out Trump on 24.3%. The second surprise was how effectively the field already appeared to have winnowed itself of so-called Establishment candidates. The results showed how far the race had come since mid-2015: the young Florida senator Marco Rubio came in a strong third with 23.1% of the vote, with the most moneyed candidate, Jeb Bush, on a disastrous 3%. Bringing up the rear of the field, Ohio Governor John Kasich scored 2%, as did the combative New Jersey Governor Chris Christie, both of whom pointed with a shrug to low expectations.

But this halt in Trump's momentum – regained in any case a week later in New Hampshire – was not necessarily heartening if you happened to be a Republican Party member who wished your party to appeal eventually to the wider electorate in a general election. Taken together, the radical vote – Trump, Cruz and Ben Carson – easily outweighed the vote of the so-called moderate wing. The party's problems didn't stop there: we shall see in a moment that there is some doubt as to how moderate that moderate wing is.

But first, it is time to meet another member of the main cast. We do so with minor trepidation: one can't begin to fathom how radical the Republican Party has become without meeting him.

TED CRUZ, IDEOLOGUE

In Ted Cruz the Republican Party faced the second prong of a dual insurgency.

On the face of it, Cruz bore strong resemblances to previous Iowa winners Rick Santorum and Mike Huckabee. Like Huckabee and Santorum, Cruz wears his religion on his sleeve and does well with evangelicals, but he is wilier and smarter than either. Although the prospect never garnered as much press in relation to Cruz as it did with his rival Marco Rubio – perhaps because the media deemed it a much less likely outcome – Rafael Edward Cruz would also have been the first Latino president. In Iowa, Cruz in fact became the first Latino to win a presidential caucus. As so often in a teeming country, the heterogeneity of the nation expresses itself in him, but perhaps a bit too much to his own self-admiration: 'I'm Cuban, Irish, and Italian, and yet somehow I ended up Southern Baptist'.

But if Cruz is many things all at once, he is first and foremost a lawyer, and a very good one.

He is like a Dickens character adrift in time and space, and reminiscent of Mr. Vholes in *Bleak House*: 'so eager, so bloodless and gaunt,' and 'always looking at the client, as if he were making a lingering meal of him with his eyes'. He is the most intelligent candidate the Republican Party has put forward since Nixon, but Cruz's is the kind of intelligence that is born in the law, sparked by the law, and can seek no other outlet than the law. It is a tale of how far Uriah Heap-ish slickness can get you. Cruz won the 1992 North American Debating Championships, and went on to graduate *magna cum laude* from Harvard Law School. Like President Obama, he served as editor of the *Harvard Law Review*. With that record, Cruz had his pick of internships. He chose the path most certain to ingratiate himself with Conservatives, and, what cannot have been a small matter to him, the one most likely to annoy President Bill Clinton. He worked first for the National Rifle Association, and then went on to prepare materials for impeachment proceedings against Clinton following the Lewinsky scandal. By 2000, he was an unloved member of George W. Bush's team, advising the then Texas Governor on a range of legal issues, including immigration policy.

Even at this distance, you get a sense that there was a forking of ways for Cruz when working under Bush. He discovered that he wasn't liked, even among his own people. It was found that he fared poorly in teams, and he seems to this day to struggle to form friendships. George W. Bush

Fig 12. Ted Cruz. As Charles Dickens put it, 'so eager, so bloodless and gaunt'.[97]

recently told an audience of Jeb Bush donors: 'I just don't like the guy.' That sentiment never seems far from assessments of Cruz. We also have this vivid portrait, dating from 2000, from a Bush campaign veteran:

> He [Cruz] was a smart and talented guy, but completely taken with himself and his own ideas. He would offer up opinions on everything, even matters outside his portfolio. He was a policy guy, but he would push his ideas on campaign strategy. He would send memos on everything to everyone. He would come to meetings where he wasn't invited — and wasn't wanted. The quickest way for a meeting to end would be for Ted to come in. People would want out of that meeting. People wouldn't go to a meeting if they knew he would be there. It was his inability to be part of the team. That's exactly what he was: a big asshole.[98]

People like this, impervious to how they come across to others, almost always end up doing what Cruz has done – they have to go it alone. In the lead-up to May 2016's Indiana primary, former Speaker John Boehner would refer to him as 'Lucifer in the flesh'. It speaks volumes about the radicalism of Trump that this pariah would eventually be considered the party's preferred flag-bearer by many among the elites.

By 2013, Cruz had been elected a Senator for Texas. The grandiosity that couldn't find an outlet in court, where one's own opinions must be subordinated to one's client's case, easily found one in the Senate. It is not quite clear when Cruz started considering himself Cicero and Obama Caitiline, but the Senate was soon hearing speeches like this, in which Cruz railed against Obama's immigration executive orders:

> When, President Obama, do you mean to cease abusing our patience? How long is that madness of yours still to mock us? When is there to be an end of that unbridled audacity of yours, swaggering about as it does now. Do not the nightly guards placed on the Border – do not the watches posted throughout the city – does not the alarm of the people, and the union of all good men —does not the precaution taken of assembling the Senate in this most defensible place – do

not the looks and countenances of this
venerable body here present, have any
effect upon you? Do you not feel that
your plans are detected?[99]

To compare a democratically elected President
to an insane insurrectionist like Caitiline was
hyperbolic in the extreme. But by 2016, Cruz had
succeeded in bolting on this message to the
platform of a typical evangelical candidate of the
far right. Cruz made a habit of exaggeration. For
instance, he denounced the Iran nuclear deal in
similarly extravagant terms, saying that it 'will
make the Obama administration the world's
leading financier of radical Islamic terrorism'.[100]

Like Trump, he speaks an extreme
language, but unlike Trump, his extremity
is coherent. Cruz would stand or fall by the
Constitution: he considers it an essentially
static document to be vigilantly protected. The
Second Amendment is not to be changed just
because there have been regular gun massacres
these past years – it is apparently too sacred
to make way for the safer country its rewriting
would surely produce. Cruz's positions look
principled at first. On inspection they are
doggedly anti-Enlightenment, and hinge on a

fierce refusal to take facts into account. On climate change, for instance, he will speak obliquely about satellite data disproving the existence of human-caused climate change. He will state that the planet hasn't warmed for 17 years, selectively choosing a figure that backs the political position he wants to take. He can sound plausible even while taking up a radical point of view. He would not permit abortion even in cases of incest or rape, and announced his candidacy at Liberty University, where a creationist view of the world is central to the syllabus. Among the candidates, there is none so eager to do away with Obamacare: in October of 2013, he aimed to shut down the government in a bid to convince the President to defund his own health program. This was a non-starter from the beginning, but it says a lot about Cruz that he continued with it anyway. Perhaps he was simply trying to make his name. More likely, he believed his plan could work.

The Cruz candidacy, one should add, was scary to plenty of Republicans. In hindsight, it's possible to see that the presence of Cruz in the field blinded some in the party to Trump. The more the Republican Party looked at Cruz, the more they started to think of Trump as a political innocent who might be coached. For instance,

The New York Times reported the following encounter with the 1996 Republican nominee Bob Dole:

> 'When I question his allegiance to the party,' Mr. Dole said of Mr. Cruz. 'I don't know how often you've heard him say the word "Republican" — not very often.' Instead, Mr. Cruz uses the word "conservative," Mr. Dole said, before offering up a different word for Mr. Cruz: "extremist."[101]

The piece goes on to report Dole as saying that Trump could 'probably work with Congress because he's, you know, he's got the right personality and he's kind of a deal-maker.' We do not yet know how costly this error might be. But at a certain point in time powerful people in the Republican Party decided that Trump was biddable and that Cruz was not. They did so on the assumption that there would be enough time to pivot to a moderate candidate once Cruz had been finished off. Others honestly preferred Cruz and backed the wrong horse.

There is no difficulty in imagining what a Cruz administration would have looked like:

it would have been the most radical Republican administration in history. Government departments would have closed; the market would have again been deregulated; the Iran deal have would been torn up; and there would have been no American involvement in the fight against climate change. Much of the federal government – including the departments of energy, commerce, education, and housing and urban development – would have been rolled back. But one shouldn't breathe too much of a sigh of relief. When Cruz did eventually concede to Donald Trump in May 2016, he tweeted: 'Over the past 13 months, we built a movement. Make no mistake, that movement will continue.' He might be right about that: but for Trump, he might well have won. If Trump loses in November, a Cruz-style candidate – perhaps Cruz himself – is sure to resurface in 2020.

THE TWO-PARTY SYSTEM

Watching the Republican Party wrestle with these insurgents, one is tempted to state a fact so obvious it might otherwise be overlooked: America has an entrenched two-party system.

In a large country, national politics will

always be a tale of uneasy accommodations: an evangelical in Iowa will have little in common with a financier on Wall Street, but both might vote Republican. Likewise, not much unites a non-college educated activist in Mississippi and a college graduate in Connecticut who hasn't yet taken to the streets to combat racial injustice – except perhaps the Democratic Party. In a two-party system, there is less romance in a protest vote: in the 2016 primaries, one has the impression of a pervasive rage among blue-collar voters who consider themselves marginalised struggling to find an outlet within a system that doesn't cater to the extent of that anger. It has sometimes seemed as though a three- or even four-party politics is struggling to be born. This frustration is expressing itself through the Republican Party, but the party itself, the means of that expression, is partly the *object* of that frustration. It is a case of new and bitter wine in old bottles.

This two-party system grew up at the outset of the country's history around a difference in opinion between Federalists, as represented by Alexander Hamilton, and the Jeffersonian view, which coalesced around the Democratic-Republican Party. Jefferson explained the distinction in his 1798 letter to John Wise:

> Two political Sects have arisen within the US the one believing that the executive is the branch of our government which the most needs support; the other that like the analogous branch in the English Government, it is already too strong for the republican parts of the Constitution; and therefore in equivocal cases they incline to the legislative powers: the former of these are called federalists, sometimes aristocrats or monocrats, and sometimes Tories, after the corresponding sect in the English Government of exactly the same definition: the latter are stiled republicans, Whigs, Jacobins, anarchists, dis-organizers, etc. these terms are in familiar use with most persons.[102]

This argument about the size of government rages today, with Cruz in favour of the smallest government and the most visible (and extreme) 'republican', and Bernie Sanders (see Chapter Eight) as the most 'federalist'. As is hinted at in Jefferson's letter, the two-party system was borrowed from the United Kingdom. There were limits to the imagination of the Founding Fathers: the British two-party system had been built around an institution, the monarchy, which America had been expressly designed to escape. So the young nation had rebelled from the United Kingdom, but ended up with a political system reminiscent of the mother country's.

Interestingly, there is no mention of the idea of party in the Constitution. From that time onwards, America has divided itself, like variations upon a theme, around two factions: this has led to strange bedfellows. The undoubted low point was Nixon's southern strategy which sought to win white votes for the Republicans in the South by appealing to racist sentiment. A presidential election is really just a freeze-frame of the condition of the two-party system. At any one time each party is a broad coalition of roiling elements. In general elections, one uneasy coalition is pitted against another. In 2016, there has already been much talk of a third-party candidate on the right. It is worth remembering that these have tended to create an unintended victory for the other side – most notably Theodore Roosevelt's Bull Moose Party founded after his presidency in 1912, and Ross Perot's run as an Independent in 1992. Roosevelt's typically hyperactive run only served to hand the presidency to Wilson. Perot, espousing policies one would more associate with the Republican Party, ensured Bill Clinton's election. This is why Trump goads Sanders on Twitter on a daily basis into an independent run: a Sanders third-party candidacy would win him the election.

Is the two-party system a good thing? Some people think so. In the US, there are none of the regular switches of government that characterise, for instance, Italy with its proportional representation and larger number of parties: it has been argued that the status quo has led, in spite of numerous shocks, to broad economic stability. But the system evidently creates frustration. The heterogeneity of each party ensures that the party itself can sometimes seem either sluggish, or simply unable to satisfactorily represent certain parts of its constituency. This will sometimes express itself in protest, as with Cruz and Trump. The Democrats meanwhile have shown themselves attracted to a self-proclaimed socialist who isn't a signed-up Democrat.

In each case fundamental notions of party identity, and therefore the idea of party unity, are under threat.

WHAT IS THE REPUBLICAN PARTY 'ESTABLISHMENT'?

General elections might therefore be seen as a kind of tortuous imposition of party unity. In *The Party Decides*, an influential book published by The University of Chicago in 2008, the central thesis looks interestingly outdated in 2016:

> Parties are a systematic force in presidential nominations and a major reason that all nominees since the 1970s have been credible and at least reasonably electable representatives of their partisan traditions.[103]

This shadowy process could be seen at work with reasonable vividness in the 2012 Republican primary. In that instance, the rank-and-file of the party flirted with the idea of evangelical candidate Rick Santorum, who won over three million votes, before plumping, with notable dissatisfaction, for Mitt Romney, a centrist technocrat who looked 'presidential' and probably was the most electable option at that time. The candidate had been imposed on an unwilling party. Romney went on to lose handily, but his nomination was taken as a sign that the party apparatus – and its associated orthodoxies of tax cuts for the rich, and a limited social safety net – was in reasonable shape. In 2016, what is more noticeable about the nomination of Romney, is not the imposition itself but the underlying unwillingness. Romney, it seems, was the last straw for many.

But if candidates are regularly imposed on the rank-and-file by the establishment then the question arises: 'Who is the establishment?'

The simple answer one might expect is: rich people.

There's a fair amount of evidence to say this is so. A recent article in *The New York Times* estimated that 158 families provided nearly half of the early money in the 2016 race.[104] Of these families, only 20 supported the Democratic Party. These Republican donors tend to be self-made – the kind of dynamic earners who, like Trump, have the self-propelled momentum that doesn't stop at mere wealth and prompts them to attempt to extend their influence. A significant proportion of them belong to the finance or energy industries.

The trouble in 2016 is that they didn't speak with one voice. Many of those families supported candidates one would normally consider non-establishment: for instance, the Koch brothers, influential titans of manufacturing, threw a lot of money behind Ted Cruz. Perhaps in its way this was healthy: primary seasons ought to look like crises within the two-party system if they are to be democratic at all. But usually the Party 'decides' and rallies round a viable strategy. Donors, elected representatives in the House of Representatives and the Senate, leading evangelicals, representatives of the NRA, and powerful right-wing figures in the media like Glenn Beck or Rush Limbaugh are meant to eventually pipe down *en masse* and focus on the common enemy.

The spectacle of 2016 makes one wonder whether the arrangement has ever been as orderly as *The Party Decides* would suggest. It now looks doubtful that it was as ever as powerful as a small cabal confidently pulling the strings. Of course the Trump nomination might in the long run prove an aberration – and the sort of aberration that only an eccentric billionaire could throw up – and that normal service might be resumed in 2020. In another sense, if the party does rally round Trump, as seems to be the case at time of writing, then it might be considered a show of unity of sorts – just a much more reluctant one than usual. But this wouldn't change the fact that for now, the party emperors appear to have no clothes. It doesn't feel as though we've really witnessed a decision at all, so much as a tortured and multifarious reconciling to a chaotic process.

JEB BUSH AND MARCO RUBIO

How did this happen? In 2016 if the Republican Party establishment decided at all, it did so wrongly – twice. It plumped for Jeb Bush, George W. Bush's younger brother and a former Governor of Florida. When Bush proved disastrous, the party went for Marco Rubio, who repeated the same pattern.

It is difficult to recall now, but throughout the Obama years, Jeb Bush had been a whispered-about and thrilling prospect to many Republicans and even to some independents. Seeing this, and scenting a familial right, Bush entered the race and by October of 2015 had raised $128 million, some $103 million of that through the unlimited super-PAC model, which we saw endorsed by the *Citizens United* decision earlier. This was more even than Hillary Clinton had raised.

Thus began the Bush campaign (or Jeb! 2016). Bush was celebrated as a 'policy wonk' and is still considered cerebral in some quarters. And it is true that he has defended Obama against Trump's wilder claims. He has also taken a comparatively moderate line on immigration, supporting a path to 'earned legal status', although not to citizenship. On the other hand, to be moderate alongside Trump and Cruz is not in any normal sense to be moderate. Bush's failed candidacy provides a useful case study into how far to the right the Republican Party has gone. Bush would have repealed Obamacare, thus denying millions healthcare, and replaced it with a tax credit. He talked of 'phasing out' Medicare. He cast himself as a staunch opponent of federal gun laws. He emphasised his friendship with the energy lobby and had this to say on climate change: 'I don't think the science is clear on what percentage is man-made and...what percentage is natural.

It's convoluted. And for the people to say the science is decided on this is just really arrogant.'[105]

The Bush campaign proved to be among the most miserable in modern history. Throughout, he was subjected to ridicule by Trump as a 'low-energy candidate' and managed to look bullied by the billionaire throughout the primary season. Ruffled, Bush tried to tack right, and raised the so-called 'anchor babies' issue – a term referring to babies born in the US to non-citizens. He had hoped to seem tough on immigration, but when this backfired, he attempted an apology: 'Frankly, it's more related to Asians.' More incredibly, he failed to come up with a plausible view of his brother's invasion of Iraq, at times seeming defiant about the original decision to invade, and at others apologetic. His solution to the wages crisis was to talk in quasi-Trump terms of a mystical 4% GDP growth he would somehow engender as president: the average growth of GDP over the last 40 years has been 2.79%.[106] Throughout the process, he failed to speak his mind; the impression was that he was too scared to do so before an electorate more radical than he is. The establishment candidate could no longer plausibly play the game. He also came to embody the fact that no amount of money can make an unlikeable candidate likeable. Bush was like an equivalent of a much-promoted film no one goes to see – the political version of Kevin Costner's *Waterland*.

Bush's poor performances leading up to that 3% finish in Iowa meant that the establishment had to cast around for another nominee. They already had their man in Marco Rubio.

By early February 2016, it looked like Rubio had a serious shot at the nomination: young, apparently beloved by the establishment, and moving into more promising electoral territory post-Iowa, one imagined that he might be the man to eat into Trump's lead. Rubio was born to Cuban immigrants who were naturalised in 1975. Like Obama, both Clintons, and Cruz, Rubio studied law. He rose through the state legislature to become speaker of the Florida House of Representatives, a position he held until November of 2008, the month of Obama's election. As much as he professes to despise Obama, Rubio's career closely shadows his. By 2010, Rubio was a Senator, a position he juggled with teaching at Florida International

University – he would often have to answer allegations that he had been a somewhat absentee lawmaker. Still, Rubio was a young Latino in an organisation that desperately needed to appeal to that constituency. Around this time, he became of value to a party elite that had drawn the conclusion that Romney's 2012 defeat had been caused not by the party's stated tax position, but by the Republican position on immigration. In 2013, Congressional Republicans formed the so-called Gang of Eight, which aimed to pass bipartisan immigration reform. The goal was to neutralise the issue and make Florida, with its 29 Electoral College votes, winnable again. Rubio was a member of the Gang: a path to citizenship was touted and, as we saw in Chapter Four, nothing passed. But Rubio was already spoken of as a viable presidential candidate.

Like Jeb Bush, Rubio in 2016 often seemed unsure of his ground. He was also outflanked by Trump on immigration, and publicly moved away from the comprehensive immigration reform he had apparently espoused as a member of the Gang of Eight. He came to favour a step-by-step approach with the emphasis on border enforcement. It was hard not to see this as a betrayal of his previous claim that immigration is 'a law and order issue but it's also a human issue'.[107] Voters could tell that Rubio wasn't being honest with them: they preferred Trump's bluntness to this kindlier hedging. He also disputed the science on climate change, and pledged to scrap Obama's Clean Power Plan. Like Bush, Rubio planned to undo Obamacare and replace it with a tax credit. On economics, he also espoused orthodoxy – tax cuts for the rich – and was outflanked by Trump who appealed to the disenfranchised blue-collar voter. Rubio had voted against the stimulus package and favoured deregulation – if a 2008-style recession were to happen again, Rubio would presumably have let the system 'self-correct' in defiance of the Keynesian position. Rubio opposed gun control. On foreign policy, he was hawkish on Iran and stated that he would re-impose sanctions from day one. He also talked of sending troops into Iraq and Syria.

In every regard, a Rubio presidency would have looked a lot like the Bush presidency – except that the Bush administration was arguably more moderate in favouring immigration reform, and in passing TARP. Rubio, spun in the media as a moderate, was anything but. But like Cruz, he is young and may run again one day. At the time of exiting the race, Rubio was running neck-and-neck, or slightly ahead, of Hillary Clinton in most head-to-head match-ups.

After his strong third-place finish in Iowa, Rubio gave a poor debate performance in New Hampshire, during which his slick style was bullishly mocked by Chris Christie. Bush dropped out after South Carolina; Rubio's defeat to Trump in his home state of Florida in turn sealed his fate. The Republican primary – which had started with 17 candidates – came to resemble a version of Agatha Christie's *And Then There Were None*. Some party moderates turned wearily and with little hope to Ohio Governor John Kasich. Others began to feel that Cruz was their best bet – at least, unlike Trump, he was a conservative. Kasich did manage to win his home state of Ohio, but elsewhere continually came in third after Trump and Cruz. His candidacy nevertheless had a comparative decency about it. On Obamacare, he initially said repeal was 'never going to happen'. This made him so unpopular that he eventually fell in line and said it would indeed happen. On climate change, he observed that it is a problem, although it has also been noted that his record on fracking as Governor has been decidedly mixed. Kasich was moderate also on same-sex marriage. There was a streak of realism about Kasich: if there is any truth in *The Party Decides*, then one would have expected it to have decided in his favour.

The Bush, Rubio, and Kasich candidacies all pointed to the same fact. Each seemed palatable when standing next to Cruz or Trump, but each stood for a Republican Party that has moved far to the right. A significant portion of the Republican electorate was simply too angry with Washington and with business-as-usual to accept moderate politicians. In the end, a loss in Indiana did for both Cruz and Kasich. Kasich's campaign had become undeniably quixotic by the end: he stayed in the race in the hope of emerging victorious in a contested convention in Cleveland. In the event of losing the nomination under those circumstances, Trump had hinted that there would be riots: perhaps it is preferable that he be defeated democratically in November.

In hindsight, Trump's win was a ruthlessly logical conclusion to that first day of Obama's administration when the Republicans had met on the Hill and pledged to oppose the new President no matter what. At that point, they became untethered from reality: and they ended up with a reality TV star as a result. It is as if real life had migrated into television, and only there could it find some resolution. The outcome of this primary was a just punishment for the decision to co-govern so petulantly.

And so in a few short months of angry insults, riots, childishness and limited policy discussion, the Republican Party had created an America in which Donald Trump – pugilist, braggart, entertainer, bigot, neo-fascist – was a step away from the presidency.

Who stands in his way, and what party does she belong to?

PART IV

THE DEMOCRATS IN 2016

CHAPTER 7 – HILLARY RODHAM CLINTON

Look, I've said how much I admire Hillary's toughness, her smarts, her policy chops, her experience. You've got to admit it, though, Hillary trying to appeal to young voters is a little bit like your relative just signed up for Facebook. (Laughter.) "Dear America, did you get my poke?" (Laughter.) "Is it appearing on your wall?" (Laughter.) "I'm not sure I am using this right. Love, Aunt Hillary." (Laughter and applause.) It's not entirely persuasive.

– President Obama at the 2016 White House Correspondents' Dinner

While all this was going on in the Republican Party, the Democratic Party returned some surprising Iowa caucus results of its own. The results saw Hillary Clinton just edge out self-described democratic socialist Bernie Sanders by a fraction of the vote. The surprise of this was two-fold. In the first place, Hillary had started out with enormous advantages in funding, name recognition and Democratic Party endorsements. And Sanders, at 74, was an unlikely challenger not just because of his age – he would have been the oldest president to take the oath – but also because 'socialism' has long been a dirty word in American life. A week later, Sanders went on to score a large victory in New Hampshire, winning 61% to Hillary's 39%. Clinton would rebound, winning strong support among blacks and Latinos in the South – her so-called firewall. This included a 73.4% win in South Carolina. But Sanders' subsequent win in Michigan ranks as one of the greatest upsets in modern political history: he overturned a substantial Clinton poll lead to win 49.8% to 48.3%.

Once again, as on the Republican side, pundits were left asking the question: How did this happen? There are political and economic reasons which we shall look at in the next Chapter. But politics is also about personality – and as important, the perception of personality.

And so we need to talk about Hillary.

PERCEPTIONS OF HILLARY

Hillary Rodham Clinton is one of the most famous women on the planet. She has topped Gallup's poll for most admired woman 20 times,[108] and has the highest name recognition, along with Donald Trump, in the 2016 race.[109] In spite of these facts, she suffers from a common ailment among celebrities: to be known is not always to be liked, and even to be liked not necessarily to be loved. She can inspire admiration, but she doesn't excite. Sometimes her predicament can seem more dramatic than this: without committing any known crimes, and while campaigning continually for children's and women's rights for half a century, she has somehow become the most hated woman in America. Among modern politicians, Clinton most resembles former UK Prime Minister Gordon Brown. There is the same alleged gap, attested by friends, between how she apparently comes across in private and how she is perceived by the public. Like Brown, she was beaten to the leadership by a charismatic rival and may also be condemned to be that rival's successor, and a mere political afterthought, towards the tail end of her party's natural span in government.

She has undoubted weaknesses and has never been short of enemies to opine and enlarge upon them. Given her prominence, she has had fewer champions than might have been expected. She has undoubtedly suffered from being awkward and tense before the media. Kate McKinnon's impersonations on *Saturday Night*

Live – everybody now knows the mad laugh and power-hungry eyes – would not be so funny if there weren't some truth there. Also close to the mark was a recent headline on satirical news website *The Onion*: 'Hillary Clinton To Nation: "Do Not Fuck This Up For Me". In both cases, her desire for power is being mocked – and two runs at the Presidency, on top of her time as Secretary of State, Senator for New York and her period as First Lady, prove that she does indeed gravitate towards positions of power. But then the gravitation toward power is true of everyone in the 2016 race, and indeed of every president in history: if that were disqualifying, America would have to come up with some other form of government.

Her faults are well-known: she isn't trusted – especially by young voters. Her recent problems over her decision to set up a private e-mail server while Secretary of State – ascribed to carelessness by Clinton herself and to an appetite for crime by her enemies – are part of a general pattern. She has also exhibited a tendency to lie during her career – usually out of personal insecurity, and to bolster herself. For instance during the 2008 race for the Democratic nomination, she made the following claims about a visit to Bosnia in 1996:

> I remember landing under sniper fire.
> There was supposed to be some kind of
> a greeting ceremony at the airport, but
> instead we just ran with our heads down
> to get into the vehicles to get to our
> base.[110]

This turned out not to be true – footage would subsequently show her arriving in apparent calm. This sort of fibbing is analogous to the self-aggrandisements people project onto their CVs. Under pressure, Clinton can lack a level head.

But if Clinton's weaknesses have been exhaustively discussed, then it must also be said that her virtues have often been cheerfully ignored – both by Republicans who would claim that she has none, and by many Democrats who see her as part of her husband's treacherous policy of triangulation – that is, of carrying on essentially Reagan-like domestic policies under the banner of a Democratic administration, which we glanced off in Chapter Two. Harsh verdicts have often come to her from unexpected quarters. When Andrew Sullivan left off his blog *The Daily Dish* saying that he couldn't bear the thought of covering the Clintons again on a daily basis, he was referring as much to the culture of grievance and response that has grown up around the Clintons as to the faults of Clinton herself.[111] Christopher Hitchens' *No One Left To Lie To* is a vitriolic attack not just on her husband, but also on Hillary, and he accuses her at the very least of turning a blind eye to sexual assaults he alleged her husband to have committed. Her tendency towards own goals can be frustrating to journalists condemned to cover them. In a 2008 *Slate* article, citing the false story peddled by then Senator Clinton that she had been named after the explorer Edmund Hillary, Hitchens complained:

> For Sen. Clinton, something is true if it validates the myth of her striving and her 'greatness' (her overweening ambition in other words) and only ceases to be true when it no longer serves that limitless purpose. And we are all supposed to applaud the skill and the bare-faced bravado with which this is done.[112]

The Hitchens indignation was always entertaining, but sometimes strained. The reference to 'overweening ambition' is reminiscent of the endless comparisons Clinton received from Republicans at the outset of her husband's 1993 administration to Lady Macbeth. Yet her supporters see her principally as 'a tough woman' who 'gets things done'. There is some truth in those descriptions, but they are clichés that don't get you near the real woman.

To an unusual degree, our ideas about Hillary – both negative and positive – are based on caricature.

TWO HILLARYS

This is partly because the life of Hillary Rodham Clinton sometimes appears to proceed along a dual track: she is both Hillary Rodham, the young idealist, and Hillary Clinton the woman who was married to the 42nd President of the United States.

Hillary *Clinton* everybody knows. It is her public self, the one voters see and don't quite warm to. She is resilient but 'robotic'; she has staying power in a man's world, but is somehow uninspiring. This side of her has repeatedly compromised, makes well-remunerated speeches at Goldman Sachs whose transcripts she won't release, and sometimes appears to take non-progressive positions, such as her slow embrace of same-sex marriage, or her vote to authorise the invasion of Iraq. This side of her seems to stem from the life she chose with her husband. After Bill Clinton enters her story there is a marked change of tone: not to overglamorise Bill, but it is as if Lord Byron had suddenly walked on stage in a drama that hadn't expected him. Indeed, it's interesting to note that forty years or so ago, Hillary Rodham, as

Fig 13. Hillary Rodham.[113]

Fig 14. Hillary Rodham *Clinton*.[114]

she was then, wavered over her marriage to Bill.
And there's a lot in the story of her life with
Bill to make you wonder whether she might
have been better off wavering some more. How
would Hillary have fared had she not followed
Bill Clinton to Arkansas in 1974, and instead
remained in Washington under the direction

of Democratic activist Betsey Wright? It's impossible to know. In January 2017 she may take the oath of office as the first female President of the United States, but even if she does, it's conceivable that she might have achieved a Hillary Rodham administration on her own, and possibly sooner. Clinton's explanation given in her memoir: 'I chose to follow my heart instead of my head'[115] has a tragic tint given the misery it would cause her. Her political career has been presented as a mere aspect of her marriage, as if she had no political life before him, which is quite false. Initially, in the heady days of 1992, Bill Clinton saw her as an asset and campaigned under the slogan 'two-for-the-price-of one'. But this time, with Bill increasingly unpredictable and sometimes ill-tempered on the campaign trail, it seems that the opposite state of affairs must be endured: 'one-for-the-price-of-two'.

To assess her suitability for the presidency, one needs to know what she was like before, without him. If she does win the presidency, Bill Clinton won't always be in the room with her.

HILLARY RODHAM

Clinton was born to Republican parents in 1947. Until 1965, when she was 18, she identified herself as a Rockefeller Republican – that is to say, she grew up in a Republican Party unrecognisable from today's which espoused moderate government investment in healthcare and New Deal-style programs. In 1960, her father Hugh cast an unlovely 1960 vote for Richard M. Nixon.

In 1965 she switched, and it's worth noting her age at this time: Clinton has been obsessively passionate about politics for half a century. This is one of her weaknesses of course: there is the perception that she knows nothing beyond politics. There is no equivalent in Hillary's life to Obama's love of basketball, her husband's playing the saxophone, or even FDR's stamp collection. Hillary went over to the Democrats for two reasons: Vietnam and the civil rights movement. She understood that the Republican Party, bogged down Iraq-style in the first and sluggish about the second, was on the wrong side of both issues. You could also say that the transformation began with a handshake: in 1962 she was taken back stage to meet Martin

Luther King Jr. after the great preacher had delivered his sermon in Chicago warning against 'sleeping through the revolution'.

Hillary Rodham didn't sleep through it. For the next decade, she embarked on a life of restless activism, almost always on behalf of children and women. The civil rights movement and the movement for women's rights went hand in hand for Hillary Rodham: she was a strong proponent of Title VII of the Civil Rights Act, which prohibits discrimination on the basis of gender. America still thinks of her primarily as her husband's wife: all along, she was a force of nature in her own right. Hillary was active in politics at an age when most people don't know what politics entails. Even before she was stung out of the Republican Party – and there is no reason to disbelieve her that her conscience drove her out – in 1969, at the age of 22, she was already working to bring more black students into Wellesley College in the wake of the assassination of Dr. King. She can point to a lifelong loathing of racism.[116]

There can't be many people alive today who have done more for the welfare of children than Hillary Rodham Clinton: it is an impossible-to-ignore leitmotif of her life. She entered Yale Law School and straightaway joined the Yale Child Center and there studied brain development in young children. At that time, she took on child abuse cases at Yale-New Haven Hospital. In her summers, she interned, not at a corporate firm as her image today prepares you to expect, but at a firm specialising in constitutional rights, so that she could handle child custody cases. Over time, she would become one of the country's leading experts in children's rights. She served while a postgraduate as staff attorney to the Children's Defense Fund in Massachusetts, and worked pro bono in child advocacy throughout the 1970s. Years later, during her husband's administration, she would be a crucial force in the passage of the Children's Health Insurance Program, which provided health insurance to six million children, and which we saw expanded in the early days of the Obama presidency in Chapter Four. During her husband's administration, she also secured funding for research into childhood asthma from the National Institute of Health. Neither the Adoption and Safe Families Act nor the Foster Care Independence Act – also important legislation passed during her husband's administration – would have happened without her involvement.

None of this is quite the record of a soulless robot. Advocacy for women represents another facet of her career and would likely form an important aspect of her presidency. During her husband's first term, Hillary was active in encouraging women to seek mammograms in order to detect breast cancer. She helped initiate the Office on Violence Against Women. Her concern for women doesn't stop at her own borders: Clinton spoke out throughout the 1990s against the Taliban's treatment of women, and also helped create Vital Voices, which has assisted more than 14,000 women leaders across over 144 countries since 1997.[117] Her votes in favour of the invasions of Afghanistan and Iraq were both conducted with the rights of women in mind. Her time as Secretary of State continued this work: the so-called 'Hillary Doctrine' refers to her view – surely a correct one – that there is a direct correlation between those countries that treat women violently or unequally, and those countries which tend to pose a threat to the United States.

Try as one might, it is hard to read any of this cynically. It is a record of substantial and meaningful achievement.

But at the same Hillary Rodham also became Hillary Rodham *Clinton*.

HILLARY RODHAM CLINTON

At first, becoming Hillary Rodham Clinton had a great deal to do with embarking on a trajectory towards wealth.

In Arkansas, where she moved in order to be with Bill, Hillary gradually accumulated riches. As the first female partner at Rose Law Firm, her salary would remain bigger than Bill's all the way to the White House. In addition to this, she did exceptionally well out of cattle-futures trading in the late 1970s. And of course, since Bill's elevation to the presidency, money has never been a serious problem: Hillary herself can now command $200,000 per speech. Bill meanwhile can charge as high as $750,000. Hillary in 2016 is worth around $31 million, the Clintons together are worth $111 million.

Her life became inescapably corporate in look and feel. We have already seen Donald Trump donating money to her. In 2016, she still accepts many large 'Wall Street' donations: an air of compromise hangs over her. Sometimes one sees a fruitful interplay between the two selves: Clinton took a position on the board of Wal-Mart, but the Rodham in her forced them to improve their environmental standards. But one often senses unease: Hillary Rodham Clinton's support for the Iraq War lumped her together with Bush and Cheney et al., increasing her resemblance to the very people Hillary Rodham had apparently dedicated herself to fighting during the Vietnam War. These things, together with her association with her husband's sometimes right-wing policies – including mass incarceration and the signing of the North American Free Trade Agreement (which she did privately oppose), 'Don't Ask Don't Tell', and the Defence of Marriage Act have twice made her vulnerable to an attack from the left: by Barack Obama in 2008, and from Bernie Sanders in 2016. Today, she looks uncomfortable with all these policies, and it is never clear whether this discomfort is caused by her having gone against her true self in espousing them, or because she now knows that they're unpopular and losing her votes. Either she must regret the expediency of her younger self, or wish that her expediency had been smarter. Another possible cause of Hillary's unpopularity is that one is never quite sure which.

Had Hillary not married Bill, her life would have been different. There would have been no Starr Report – at least not with her as a lead role in the drama. There would have been no comparisons to Lady Macbeth. The names Monica Lewinsky, Gennifer Flowers, Kathleen Willey, Paula Jones, and Juanita Broaddrick would never have caused her pain. The entire issue of Bill Clinton's affairs is grubby and opaque: one feels one knows more about it than one would like. No fair assessment should ignore that a huge amount was done to Hillary that she has every right to be angry about. Bill Clinton certainly had affairs – Lewinsky and Flowers have stated that they were consensual. Jones claims that Clinton exposed himself and propositioned her in 1991: Clinton settled an $850,000 suit with her, admitting no guilt, though the reliability of her case isn't helped by her attachment to conservative movement lawyers. Willey claims the 42nd President of the United States groped her at the White House: she was deemed an unreliable witness by independent counsel when it emerged she had expressed to a friend a previous romantic interest in Clinton. Broaddrick, most seriously, claims that Clinton raped her in 1978, but her story has changed many times in the 40 years or so since the alleged incident. It isn't clear what Hillary did or didn't do; to this day, allegations abound – in

2016, both Broaddrick and Jones have reiterated their allegations – that Hillary was more zealous than she should have been in digging up dirt on her husband's accusers. None of this has been proven, and it should be remembered that unfair allegations against Hillary have been common throughout her public life. One suspects she has been caught up in a maelstrom made up of her husband's affairs and the exceptionally partisan atmosphere in which those affairs surfaced.

Her difficulties are partly the result of the sheer conflict and longevity of her public life. Everything that has been written on Clinton has amounted to a perfect conspiracy to obscure her: the biographer labours under a surfeit of information. She is like the *Mona Lisa* – well-known, but few really bother to look at her anymore. She has been partly responsible for the fatigue: hurt led to self-protective secrecy and its offshoot, banal coverage. This also must be said in mitigation. In spite of many attempts to paint her marriage as one purely of convenience, Hillary Clinton has also, surely, had her heart broken in public, and been forced to watch while others found it amusing. The experience is vividly told in a recent book *The Residence*:

White House Florist Ronn Payne remembers one day during the Clinton presidency when he was coming up the service elevator with a cart to pick up old floral arrangements and saw two butlers gathered outside the West Sitting Hall listening in as the Clintons argued viciously with each other. The butlers motioned him over and put their fingers to their lips, telling him to be quiet. All of a sudden he heard the first lady bellow "goddamn bastard!" at the president – and then he heard someone throw a heavy object across the room. The rumor among the staff was that she threw a lamp. The butlers, Payne said, were told to clean up the mess.[118]

If there is real pain behind that 'Goddam bastard', then there must also be real dignity in her ability to have survived that time.

Survive she did. Since 2000, one gets the impression of someone who could never leave politics alone even if she wanted to. As Senator for New York, she initially kept a low profile, preferring to build relationships with fellow lawmakers. In the wake of the September 11th attacks, she helped secure $21.4 billion in order to redevelop the World Trade Center site. But she also ended up casting unwise votes in favour of the Iraq War and the Patriot Act, which would go a long way toward costing her the Democratic nomination in 2008. We shall look at her role as Secretary of State in the Obama administration in a moment. But by 2016, Clinton almost seems to have outlived the historic nature of her own possible election. Her ascendance to the presidency would be as ground-breaking in its way as Obama's, and yet the glass ceiling she would be smashing is already cracked a fact which is to some extent of her own causing.

WHAT WOULD PRESIDENT CLINTON DO?

Today Clinton exhibits less entitlement than she did in 2008, but instead a considerable preparedness for the presidency. She should do: she would be the most qualified candidate for the office since Richard Nixon. This in itself, isn't necessarily a heartening comparison, but the fact remains she has been active in politics all her life, for much of it at the very highest levels.

It is noticeable compared with the

Republican candidates how comfortable she is with nuance and detail. Her campaign has been notably substantive: she has provided easily the most detailed policy analysis of any of the candidates in either party. Clinton might campaign in prose, but that at least makes it possible for voters to say what she would likely do. In reality, with American politics as entrenched and divided as it is, it is possible that even with a substantial Electoral College victory against Trump, her election would not generate the kind of nationwide ardour that can create the mood of sweeping change necessary to affect local voting enough to flip the Senate and House to her advantage. Even if a third-party, right-leaning candidate were to emerge, splitting the conservative vote, congressional elections, which are determined by local issues, would still likely deprive her of the kind of friendly Congress Obama had for his first two years or so. She will probably end up governing with an obstructionist Senate and Congress as her husband and Obama have had to do at various points of their presidencies.

On the economy, Clinton has placed the issue of wages at the centre of her campaign. Her website states: 'Hillary understands that in order to raise incomes, we need strong growth, fair growth, and long-term growth'.[119] This might sound banal, but it is an important emphasis. President Obama has grown the economy; Hillary Clinton has pledged to grow it more equitably.

Clinton would aim to incent companies to share their profits with workers. She proposes a two-year 15% tax credit for companies that share profits in addition to giving pay rises. The tax credit would be capped to avoid larger companies taking advantage of the tax break. She has stated that profits would need to be widely shared. The plan would be paid for by the closing of tax loopholes, an implementation of the so-called Buffett Rule, as put forward in Obama's 2011 tax plan, which states that all millionaires should pay a minimum rate of tax of 30%. It's harder for her to make this case given her ties to Wall Street, and she doesn't make it from the gut as her rival Bernie Sanders does. But unlike Trump, and the rest of the GOP field, on everything from taxation to healthcare, she has done her sums.

Not that she has been immovably confident on policy; she initially stated that she would raise the federal minimum wage to $12, but was outflanked by Sanders who pledged to raise it to $15. By April, the Fight for Fifteen movement had gathered sufficient momentum in New York and California – both at the time upcoming primary states – that Clinton felt sufficiently pressurised to shift her position to endorse the $15 minimum wage. Mainstream economists still tend to worry that this is a too-dramatic hike which might negatively affect the unemployment rate, particularly among the 16-30 age bracket. But to put this in some perspective, Jeb Bush, that apparent moderate, wanted no federal minimum wage at all. Trump's remarks on the minimum wage have been so contradictory that it is impossible to know his position: most likely he doesn't himself know.

Hillary Clinton also favours organisations like the Consumer Financial Protection Bureau, the Securities and Exchange Commission and the Commodity Futures Trading Commission to be independently funded to stymie current Republican attempts to obstruct their work. She would also extend the statute of limitations on financial crimes from five to ten years: 'No one should be too big to jail.'[120] Clinton's plans, in their quiet way, are radical, and certainly to the left of President Obama's.

This isn't really surprising. Liberals tend to build on whatever government programs are in place to make them work better. This can always be called moving to the left, when really the imagery is wrong: it is a case of tweaking the existing structures. In response to hearing one of her economics speeches at New School in July 2015, Michael Tomasky, admittedly a strong supporter of Clinton's, wrote:

> If a relatively unknown Democratic governor of Illinois or Michigan were running for president, and he gave the speech Hillary Clinton gave Monday morning at the New School, rank-and-file liberals would be turning rapturous cartwheels.[121]

But they don't turn cartwheels because of their distaste for Clinton as messenger. Their distaste, however, doesn't mean she wouldn't try to accomplish her stated goals. Clinton's plan is backed by economists, including Federal Reserve Vice-Chairman Alan Blinder of Princeton University and Laura D. Tyson. Her campaign page provides numerous links to academic discussion. Throughout their campaigns, neither Marco Rubio's nor Jeb Bush's 'jobs' page had any links or references. Meanwhile, Trump, in a move ludicrous even for him, proposed removing income tax on anyone single earning less than $25,000, or on married couples jointly earning less than $50,000, and the creation of a new one-page form to send to the IRS which simply says: 'I win'.

Clinton's economic plan forms part of a bigger picture. Across a range of policy issues, she focuses on affordability. The implication is that Obama has introduced a series of just reforms which now need to be made cost-effective for working families.

For instance, a President Clinton would keep Obamacare in place, but she would also aim to make prescription drugs more affordable. It is another evidence-based policy. The average senior will spend $500 a year on medicines, and the figure will be much higher for those who happen to have chronic conditions. Meanwhile, the pharmaceuticals industry enjoys profits of $80-90 billion – money which a President Clinton would prefer to be spent on research and development. She would require health insurance plans to cap prescription drugs costs at $250, and also encourage competition within the pharmaceuticals industry by speeding up the multi-year generic drug approval backlog. Interestingly, Trump proposes something similar. But the Republican Party in general is confused on the issue. Rubio, for instance, accused the pharmaceutical companies of 'pure profiteering', but he laced this populist position – presumably designed to pick off some Trump voters – with the claim that the rise in prices is linked to the slow process by which generic drugs gain regulatory approval. It is another policy vacillation and shows that the Republican movement supports policies that will lead to inequality so as to appeal to its donor base, but that it would rather nobody knew that this is its position.

In pledging a cap on drugs costs, and in calling for higher rebates for prescription drugs within the Medicare program, Clinton is again building on the Obama years. Of course she can't campaign, as he did, on the thrilling promise of universal healthcare as an American right, since, in principle, this has already been demonstrated. The Republicans in general – and in spite of numerous contradictory statements, this goes for Trump too – continue to campaign on the grabbing promise to repeal it. On healthcare, as with Wall Street Reform, Clinton faces a difficulty she didn't face in 2008. The incremental nature of what she wants to do plays into her apparent weaknesses as a campaigner. Obama introduced the Affordable Healthcare Act; Clinton would tweak it so that insurers and employers would be required to provide up to three sick visits to a doctor per year without needing to meet the plan's deductible first. Important as that would be for the many toiling under rising deductibles and stagnant wages, it is difficult to explain it, let alone make it sound exciting. One suspects that not even JFK in his prime could set the crowds roaring with that one – but then he would have been anxious to campaign on something more grabbing.

On education, Clinton espouses the somewhat boringly-named New College Compact. For a price tag of $350 billion over ten years – paid for out of higher taxes for the rich – this initiative aims to offer free tuition for two-year programs at community colleges, and also extends subsidies to help students attend four-year programs at public universities. None of this sounds desperately thrilling when set against Bernie Sanders' cry of free college tuition for all. Legitimate debate surrounds the proposals, which echo the tuition fees debates in the UK during the Blair administration: who should pay for higher education, students or taxpayers? Clinton and – to a greater extent – Sanders have been accused of purveying Santa Claus politics, but again the Urban-Brookings Tax Policy Center found that Clinton's plans were the most carefully costed of all candidates across both parties. It is still not clear where she comes down on the debates about school reform. Does she continue to espouse the view she held in the 1990s that standards among teachers need to be raised and charter schools encouraged? Or will she come down on the side of the unions, place emphasis on public schools, and 'fight for teachers'? Caught in a tough race, and needing union endorsements, she has so far been tongue-tied on this issue. But overall, Clinton's education proposals are a world away from her Republican opponents'. At the time of writing, Donald Trump still has no 'education' tab on the Positions section of his website: he has secured the Republican nomination without showing any real interest in this important area. Cruz, with his usual thrilling radicalism, called for the abolition of the Department of Education, which would endanger federal student aid, making him to the right of George W. Bush once more.

On climate change, Clinton has pledged to have more than half a million solar panels installed by the end of her first term. She states that this initiative would increase overall solar capacity by 700%. She also speaks in vague terms of a 'Clean Energy Challenge' that will form new partnerships with states, cities, and rural communities that are 'ready to lead'.[122] This sounds interesting in principle, but is less extensive than either Sanders' plan or the plan mooted by her other, now long-forgotten challenger Martin O'Malley: O'Malley, for instance, called for a plan of 100% renewable energy by 2050. It is puzzling that Clinton hasn't gone further on an area which she has called 'an urgent challenge that threatens us all'. Clinton often campaigns with a you-can't-have-it-all tone, which is easy to outmanoeuvre. In the first quarter of 2016, she didn't care to elaborate, and at time of writing still hasn't. It is an area where she ought to do more.

Still, her approach is based on a commitment to science, which isn't the case with Trump ('a total hoax'), and wasn't the

case with Bush ('global warming may be real'),
Rubio ('We're not going to make America a
harder place to create jobs in order to pursue
policies that will do absolutely nothing, nothing
to change our climate'), Ben Carson ('There's
always going to be either cooling or warming
going on'), Chris Christie ('It's not a crisis'), and
Ted Cruz who rails against 'partisan dogma and
ideology'.

HILLARY ABROAD

In foreign policy, it is inherently more difficult
for a candidate to provide detail – most of the
challenges a president faces in this area unfold
over time, and Clinton is undoubtedly vague
when she states that she would defeat ISIS,
support Israel, hold China accountable, and
stand up to Putin. No-one can quite know in
what contexts she will be called upon to live up
to these expectations.

But in general, Clinton would keep
in place the Iran deal, and would 'vigorously
enforce the agreement'. Her record during the
Obama administration shows her to be on the
hawkish side of things, backing, for instance, the
killing of Osama bin Laden while Joe Biden was

doubtful, and arguing strongly for intervention in Libya, and even for aggressive action against China. The foreign policy establishment which Obama is proud of ignoring over Syria is not something of which she is instinctively critical. Dating back to the 1990s, she has always had friends among the generals. But she also executed the pivot to Asia and negotiated the new Strategic Arms Reduction Treaty with Russia – this should remind us that it is not a small thing that she has dealt with governments worldwide for years. The most characteristic aspect of her time at State was the emphasis she placed on women's rights around the world, and this would no doubt continue were she to become president. Most encouragingly of all, Clinton consistently illustrates a thoughtful approach. Here is a representative excerpt of an interview with Charlie Rose in 2009 in response to a question about the time it took the Obama administration to come up with a decision on troop withdrawals from Afghanistan:

> Well, I have to say that I think we went
> through eight years where, at least it
> appeared on the outside, that there
> wasn't enough time taken, there wasn't

enough thought given as to what we were trying to achieve and how we would achieve it. There were a lot of midcourse corrections. Witness the surge in Iraq. And part of what the President is trying to do with his national security team is to go and seek out information that is of direct relevance, evaluate that information, make sure that we are putting forth the best thought in order to fulfill the mission that he's going to set.[123]

Clinton's answer illustrates not just the Obama administration's evidential approach to policy-making, but also her own understanding of that approach. It is as good an indication as any of her own likely method. It is worth comparing to the emotive language used by Republican candidates. Here is Trump on waterboarding: 'I would bring it back, yes. I would bring it back. I think waterboarding is peanuts compared to what they'd do to us'. Ted Cruz: 'If you vote for me, under no circumstances will Iran be allowed to acquire nuclear weapons. And if the Ayatollah doesn't understand that, we may have to help introduce him to his 72 virgins'. Rubio again was more moderate-sounding in his language but also planned to tear up the deal with Iran and appeared unsure whether he would let Syrian refugees into the country: 'Does common sense still apply? Of course it does. A five-year-old orphan, a 90-year-old widow, a well-known Chaldean priest — these are obviously common-sense applications, and you can clearly vet them just by common sense.' Rubio seems to suggest that a parentless child is somehow less dangerous than one with parents. Again he was straining to sound more radical than he'd perhaps prefer, so as to impress the far right. As W.B. Yeats put it: 'The best lack all convention, while the worst/ are full of passionate intensity'[124].

Clinton's campaign also aims to tackle other policy issues ranging from disability rights to finding a cure for Alzheimer's. Her immigration policy would essentially be to reintroduce the DREAM Act and would favour supervised release over family detention. She would also move to close private detention centers. Comprehensive immigration reform would likely remain undone in the event of a divided Congress, although a third electoral defeat for Republicans at the presidential level might again lead to another Gang-of-Eight-style effort, particularly if the Latino vote loses Florida for the Republicans again. Unlike her opponent for the nomination, and unlike any of her potential opponents in the general election, she is also a long-standing advocate of gun control.

The overall impression is of someone whose flaws have been dwelled on, and perhaps exaggerated, but whose virtues have been skimmed over. Here is President Obama's assessment in a recent interview with *Politico*:

> [S]he's extraordinarily experienced — and, you know, wicked smart and knows every policy inside and out — [and] sometimes [that] could make her more cautious, and her campaign more prose than poetry.[125]

The mistake of caution has been repeated in 2016, but the same virtues are there. Like the Obama administration, a Clinton administration would not be perfect, but it is possible to make educated guesses at what a President Clinton would try to do (unlike a President Trump), and it would not be primarily ideological (as with a President Cruz).

Obama appears to consider Clinton his natural successor, and the early opinion polls suggest that, barring some calamity, she ought to win a one-on-one race against Trump. Yet one says this with caution, because she has made a habit of struggling to win apparently unlosable elections.

And part of one's doubts stems from the fear that some on the left will stay at home in November. Once again, in 2016, she has often seemed out of sync with the mood of her own party.

CHAPTER 8 – THE STATE OF THE LEFT IN 2016

The flaw in the pluralist heaven is that the heavenly chorus sings with a strong upper-class accent.
– Elmer Eric Schattschneider

Two things are simultaneously true about America: it teems with variety, and it is highly unequal.

The most frequently cited economic fact by the Obama administration is that unemployment has fallen from a high of 10% to 5% since the President took office. As of April 2016, it has experienced 74 consecutive months of job growth. But the news isn't all good. We have seen that this progress has been accompanied by a stagnation in wages, which has hurt median household income. Real employment is also higher than oft-cited government projections because there are many not caught by the official unemployment rate who have given up looking for work. The high numbers in prison in the US – about 1 in 100 adult Americans are behind bars – also distort the picture: many would further swell the pool of unemployed if they were released. Dry statistics give little sense of the urgency of the problem: they only hint at it. For Joseph Stiglitz, author of the defining the text on inequality, it's a matter of life and death. What could be starker than this fact:

> Decreases in income and decline in standards of living are often accompanied by a multitude of social manifestations – malnutrition, drug abuse, and deterioration in family life, all of which take a toll on life expectancy.[126]

Concealed somewhere in statistics released by the treasury are the shocking stories of our time: the dropout and the frustrated talent, starving or unprotected children, the criminal and the criminal's victim, the drug-pusher and the opioid addict. This is why such a sense of injury and violated promise permeates the 2016 race: in a land which pledges the American dream, many feel it wasn't supposed to be this way. It is a manifestation of a global problem: Stiglitz shows how the same sorts of trends have affected European countries, and have also been drivers in the Arab Spring. It is not therefore surprising that, left to speak for themselves, the 2016 Republican electorate can sometimes display a marked self-pity, and many of these people have gravitated to the Trump campaign. All this is bound up with the tremendous complication of race in America. Here, for instance, are the words of Rhett Benhoff, a middle-aged white man from North Carolina who attended a Trump rally:

> I mean, it seems like we really go overboard to make sure all these other nationalities nowadays and colors have their fair shake of it, but no one's looking out for the white guy anymore.[127]

This is both economic and racial gripe, and there is no basis whatsoever for it: Mr Benhott is describing a real problem, but has leapt to wrong conclusions regarding it. The data is insistent: the white guy in America today has less money not in relation to blacks or Latinos or Muslims but in relation to – usually – another white guy. It is true that Asian-Americans have a higher income than whites, but blacks and Hispanics – the usual object of Trumpian ire – do far worse. It is not surprising then to find a good number of people, usually with college degrees, who recognise the same problem of stagnant wages and inequality, and who didn't go to Trump. Some went instead to Clinton, but the lion's share went to Bernie Sanders.

But race also played its part in the Democratic primary. Time and again, Hillary Clinton was saved by black and Latino votes, particularly in the South. In other words, the very people who might most benefit from Sanders' more left-wing policies were not, in the end, persuaded by him.

A BRIEF HISTORY OF ECONOMIC INEQUALITY IN THE US

Economic inequality has always been a part of American life, but it wasn't always so pronounced as it is today. The 1980s were a hinge point for inequality in America, as they also were in the UK. Economists view the middle of the 20th century as a period of Great Compression in wages, a development that was caused by Roosevelt's New Deal, which was funded by progressive taxation. The Revenue Act of 1935 was derided as a 'Soak the Rich' tax at the time, and perhaps with good reason: over the next decades, it saw the percentage of income owned by the top 1% drop to beneath 10%. But inequality rose sharply under Reagan, continued under Bill Clinton, and the percentage of income owned by the top 1% reached a high of 23.5% under George W. Bush.

According to the Congressional Budget Office, for the 1979-2007 period, after-tax income of households in the top 1% of earners grew by 275%, compared to 65% for the next 19%, just under 40% for the next 60%, and 18% for the bottom fifth of households.[128] The US compounds an unequal economy with the weakest social security net in the developed world. The social safety net did expand under Lyndon Johnson's Great Society reforms in the mid-60s, bringing America Medicare and Medicaid. But over time, Milton Friedman and his adherents contended that Social Security should be privatised – Reagan, essentially a Friedmanite, was more concerned with simplifying the tax code than adding government programs. As we glanced at in Chapter Two, the Democratic Party, which might have been expected to channel FDR and address these discrepancies, became soft on inequality. President Clinton's largest bloc of donors came from Goldman Sachs.[129] Even the Clinton welfare reform package of

1996 – partly because he had lost the House, and partly because he had wanted to sound tough on welfare all along and got himself boxed into a corner – was essentially a cut for poorer families, leading to a reduction in food stamps for poor children. The inequality trend, particularly when seen through the prism of race, has also caused anomalies in the criminal justice system. It is no secret that poverty creates higher crime rates. But higher crime rates also create an atmosphere of fear, which in turn leads to repressive policing. The birth of the Black Lives Matter movement during Obama's second term has been an inevitable offshoot of this policing style.

Inequality also strikes at the very heart of democracy. Imbalance in the system can be self-perpetuating. We have seen how the 2010 *Citizens United* decision, perpetrated by a right-leaning bench, refused to place limits on independent political expenditures. Meanwhile, lobbying is routinely railed against by Democrats during election season, though little is ever done. In 1971, only 175 businesses had lobbies in Washington. By 1982, 2,445 did. There are now nearly 100,000 registered lobbyists under Obama; and it's worth $9 billion as an industry.[130]

Obama would also make some missteps, such as appointing a Raytheon lobbyist to a Pentagon post in the first days of the administration.

Nor did the issue of economic inequality quite take fire in the 2008 Obama campaign. It is true that the candidate often railed against lobbyists, and spoke of the need to get away from 'trickle-down' economics. The diversity of his donor base also caused hope for some. The usually enigmatic Bob Dylan was straightforward with *The Times*:

> Poverty is demoralizing. You can't expect people to have the virtue of purity when they are poor. But we've got this guy out there now who is redefining the nature of politics from the ground up — Barack Obama. He's redefining what a politician is, so we'll have to see how things play out. Am I hopeful? Yes, I'm hopeful that things might change. Some things are going to have to.[131]

But by the time that Lehman Brothers had collapsed, the debate was all about how to salvage the system. There was less room than we have now, with the system righted, for a more general discussion about wages. By 2016, Obama's accomplishments in steadying the economy, passing healthcare and Wall Street reform have moved the conversation.

That 'things are going to have to' of Dylan's might be said to hover over 2016.

ENTER BERNIE SANDERS

The Democratic Party had been ripe for a single-issue inequality campaign to the left of the establishment. It is not altogether surprising that in the shape of Bernie Sanders, that is what it got.

Sanders' campaign was based around a 'political revolution' against the 'billionaire

Fig 15. Bernie Sanders at a town meeting in Phoenix, Arizona, July 2015.[132]

263

class'. For a single-issue campaign, it never felt limited: this was a reflection of how large a fact economic inequality has become in American life. It was, in fact, one of the great political campaigns of modern times: rarely has such unlikely gumption gone so far. C.S. Lewis once wrote: 'I believe in Christianity as I believe that the sun has risen: not only because I see it, but because by it I see everything else.' Sanders is like this with income inequality. He sees injustice at the core. It leads him to advocate for campaign finance reform, which he can do plausibly with his donations having come in huge numbers from individuals: in the last three months of 2015, he raised $33 million, with an average donation of $27.[133] By May 2016, according to insidegov.com, he had raised $185,775,339 to Clinton's $260,920,313 – an astonishing achievement. This fund-raising model, along with his message, will likely have a legacy in future elections. He can also aspire to change Washington in the cheerful knowledge that his dislike of that town is reciprocated: Sanders had only a couple of endorsements in the House of Representatives and none in the Senate, whereas Clinton has enjoyed wide support among representatives, senators and governors throughout. Sanders has perhaps something of Cato about him – always turning up with a kind of cranky benevolence to the very Senate he has apparently devoted his life to berating.

It is impossible not to admire this man who toiled so long in politics to so little fanfare but who found his moment in this campaign. There are none of the accommodations with power and the corporate world which characterise the public life of Hillary Clinton. Sanders' critics would argue that it is easier to stay untarnished by big money as a senator for a liberal state like Vermont. But the fact remains: his campaign has sparked passion like Trump's, but it has been substantive in a way that Trump's has not. It is evidential, based on a sincere anger at the state of things: there is a world of difference between Trump's small-minded tantrums and Sanders' compassionate rage.

Just as Clinton cannot be convincingly pegged as a mere pragmatist, Sanders is not simply an idealist. His time as mayor of Burlington, Vermont was marked not by any virulently anti-business agenda but by a desire for businesses to behave responsibly and pay a living wage: one suspects that he is the sort of prickly but essentially kindly man who, once sat down at a negotiating table, trades rhetoric for pragmatism. As mayor, Sanders successfully opposed the conversion of Northgate Apartments into luxury housing.[134] His time in the House of Representatives and his time in the Senate are notable for the introduction of amendments across a range of issues, including an amendment on corporate crime accountability to the Victims Justice Act 1995; a $100 million increase in funding for community health centers in 2001; and a 2013 amendment to treat autism in military healthcare, to name only a few over a long career.[135] Sanders has illustrated a knack for working with Republicans: he worked with John McCain to overhaul the US Department of Veterans Affairs by passing the most comprehensive veterans legislation in decades. Once again, there is a stark contrast between one party and the other. Trump talks a lot about veterans; Sanders expanded their access to healthcare. Sanders isn't the pitiable political idiot the media have sought to portray him as: his life is a series of attempts to solve problems.

Again there is contrast. Among Republicans, Trump has largely *caused* problems,

Cruz presented them as simpler than they are, and Rubio, Bush et al. tried to dodge them in order to get elected.

THE SANDERS PLATFORM

Sanders pledged to raise taxes to pay for an expansion of government along the lines of the Nordic model. This would have constituted a reasonably profound alteration of the contract between individual and state – enough, surely, to have given Ted Cruz a stroke. The federal government would have been found doing things it hasn't done in America before – like provide universal college tuition or run hospitals without interference from insurance companies.

It would have been a sincere attempt to change the economic inequality problem. Sanders stated that he would break up the big banks within the first year of his administration. He ran into slight difficulty on this score in an interview with *The New York Daily News*, where he seemed uncertain as to whether he would require new legislation in order to declare a bank too big to fail, or whether that power already existed under the Obama Dodd-Frank reforms. The slip was more minor than reported in some media outlets, but it was suggestive of a weakness in his candidacy: namely, a slight tendency to skim over what had actually been achieved under Obama. Sanders would have introduced a speculation tax on Wall Street. As we saw in the previous chapter, he was ahead of Clinton in proposing a $15 federal minimum wage. There is still some doubt among economists as to the wisdom of this, with some arguing that businesses would be unable to afford it, and reduce their workforce. Sanders also pledged to rewrite all existing trade agreements – from NAFTA and PNTR to the Trans-Pacific Partnership – to make them fairer and more environmentally friendly. This was another area where Sanders influenced Clinton to his side. Clinton initially called TPP 'the gold standard in trade', and after a period of tortuous vacillation now opposes it, although not very convincingly.

In healthcare, Sanders favours a single-payer system – essentially a Medicare-for-all approach without any involvement from insurance companies. Such a system would have been broadly akin to Britain's NHS. Having witnessed the scale of the angst caused by Obamacare, it is hard not to feel that Sanders' plan, particularly embarked upon so soon after Obama's reforms, would have created an extraordinary outcry. Obama has been derided as a socialist for suggesting milder policies, although there has always been a xenophobic tint to that accusation which could not have been aimed at a white president. There are persuasive arguments that a single-payer system, although undoubtedly an upheaval after the messiness of Obamacare, would be simpler, cut out the insurance companies, and provide better healthcare for more people. It will continue to be an item at the top of liberals' wish-list until it is achieved.

Next to the single-payer system on that list will be tuition-free colleges, which Sanders planned to pay for with that speculation tax on Wall Street. The same difficulty would likely have applied there in a Sanders administration, and will apply going forwards – namely Republican intransigence, which always looks like it can be talked away during a Democratic primary, but likely cannot during a Democratic administration.

In foreign policy, Sanders would have been slightly more doveish than Clinton, and in his support for drone strikes, his vote against the

Iraq invasion, and his implementation of the Iran deal, he sounded remarkably similar to Obama. In truth, it is not his favourite area. But Sanders on foreign policy – as also on climate change, which he would tackle with the carbon tax like the one Obama couldn't get passed as we saw in Chapter Four – is an indication of the essential unity of the Democratic Party. One sometimes wonders why Sanders has been so long an independent: his independence can sometimes seem as much a matter of temperament as of political leaning.

WHAT LEGACY WILL THE SANDERS CAMPAIGN HAVE?

In spite of disagreements on the size of the social safety net and on how to pay for it, the Democratic Party seems in a more stable place than does the Republican Party. Obama recently estimated that the party agrees on 95% of issues. It didn't always seem that way in March and April, as the race seemed to tighten. At a rally in Oregon in late March, a bird landed on a podium while Sanders was speaking. Sanders called it a symbol of peace, but his more ardent supporters were inclined to see it

as a fortuitous blessing on Bernie's candidacy.
Hillary supporters meanwhile were convinced
it was just a bird. Then the rancorous New York
primary kicked into action. Sanders – somewhat
ludicrously – said Clinton wasn't qualified to
be president, and Clinton began to seem more
irritated by Sanders than by Trump. Debate
intensified over the 1994 Crime Bill, which had
contributed to mass incarceration of African-
Americans – it emerged that as a congressman
Sanders had voted for it. Tension also emerged
over the role of the South in the Democratic
Party, with Sanders appearing at one point
to denigrate the votes Clinton had won in
Southern states as having come from the most
conservative part of the country. But they call it
'silly season' for a reason: it is difficult when one
is tired from over a year of events, and when one
is so near and yet so far from victory, as Sanders
is, not to ramp up the rhetoric a bit: Clinton had
done the same in 2008.

There appears to be no serious
likelihood of the Democratic party's splitting
into a socialist party built around Sanders and
a mainstream Obama-Clinton wing. As Obama
said, the areas of agreement are too broad.
Here is Hillary Clinton writing recently in *The
Huffington Post*:

As president, I will carry forward the Democratic record of achievement. I'll defend President Obama's accomplishments and build upon them. I'll work to get incomes rising for middle-class families, make college affordable, alleviate the crushing burden of student debt, protect LGBT Americans from discrimination, preserve women's access to health care and reproductive choice, and keep America safe from threats at home and abroad. And I'll never allow the Affordable Healthcare Act to be repealed.[136]

Sanders would agree with most of that, except that he'd change the phrase 'make college affordable' to 'make college free', and although he would replace Obamacare with his Medicare-for-all plan, he wouldn't repeal it and leave little or nothing in its stead as Trump would do, and as all the other Republican candidates would have done. Aside from occasional bickering, the contest has been largely grownup. So far, there is no disagreement on the left to match that between a moderate Republican like Kasich and Tea Partier Ted Cruz. The unity of the party is underscored by a loyalty to President Obama. In early 2016 Sanders left off campaigning in Iowa to meet with the President at the White House in the week before the caucuses. Clinton campaigns on a programme that has been compared in policy terms to a hypothetical Obama third term.

It is true that there are, somewhere on the left, more extreme views – leftist equivalents of the far right. The difference is that these – such as those who would still seize the means of production, or might be inclined to negotiate with ISIS –haven't made it anywhere near the mainstream of the party, and show no real prospect of doing so. If anything, the Democratic Party might be able to expand its constituency. Leaders of the Black Lives Matter movement, which emerged in the wake of the murders of numerous young black men, has not yet been entirely persuaded by the Democratic Party: Black Lives Matter protestors have rallied at both Sanders and O'Malley events, though one would have assumed that Democrats' would be the most likely platforms to appeal to them.[137] There is a distinction to be made between true and false rage. Black Lives Matter protestors call into question a world where white police ill-treat the black population, and that is, unfortunately, a real situation. Although there remain conflicting accounts surrounding the shooting of Michael Brown by Darren Wilson in Ferguson, Missouri, no one doubts that there is much to protest. Furthermore it isn't just a problem with policing – it's a wider problem about race relations. In 2012, Trayvon Martin was murdered, and his killer, George Zimmerman, was acquitted – and then, incredibly, in May 2016, tried to auction off the gun used in the killing. Meanwhile, Trump's followers conjure a world where immigrants are taking 'our jobs' and all Muslims are 'un-American', and this is a dark fantasy. These voters have nowhere to go but the Democratic Party, unless they choose to stay at home.

All this is not to say that the Sanders campaign will have achieved nothing once it is defeated, as seems all but certain. He has already moved Clinton further to the left than she would have liked to be on a host of issues. But he has also proved that the Democratic Party – and probably America as a whole – has moved to the left of where it was in 2008. The only real reasons for his defeat were the large number of superdelegates in Clinton's column, who would have flipped his way as they did for Obama in 2008 had the election tilted further towards him; Clinton's support from voters over the age of 65 who reliably turn up at the polls, and who have remained loyal to Clinton,[138] though they are a dwindling constituency; and Sanders' failure to appeal to black and Latino voters, particularly in the South. Black voters have proven loyal to the Clintons: some remember that Toni Morrison described Bill as 'the first black president', and the Clintons also have strong ties with the Latino community. One suspects that it wouldn't take much for a candidate to run on the same programme as Sanders, but who might better navigate the electoral map of the South. But as the years of gridlock under Obama have shown, the winner would need to be governing with a favourable Congress to stand a chance of enacting a Sandersesque agenda.

This then is a brief sketch of the country – fractured on the right, with tensions on the left.

Among all this confusion, some reasonable figures have emerged, and some have stoked the fears of the modern world. They are now aligned in two camps: a reasonably healthy Democratic Party, and an angry and

confused Republican Party. Before we ask
who will win, there is another thing at stake
of enormous importance which we have only
touched on from time to time. It has to do with
the country's judiciary.

PART V

ORDER OR CHAOS?

CHAPTER 9 – A DEATH IN FEBRUARY

I am saddened to report that our colleague Justice Antonin Scalia has passed away. He was an extraordinary individual and jurist, admired and treasured by his colleagues. His passing is a great loss to the Court and the country he so loyally served.
– Chief Justice John Roberts, 15th February 2016

The International Order of St. Hubertus met on the weekend of the 13th of February, 2016, at Cibolo Creek Ranch, Texas.

The goal of the meeting of this 'true knightly order', as its website describes it, was to spend another weekend advancing its motto: *Deum Diligite Animalia Diligentes – Honoring God by Honoring His Creatures*. The Order does this is by hunting and killing them. It is also committed to conserving the environment of the animals it wishes to kill. Founded by the notable 18th century patron of the arts Count Franz Anton Von Spruck, the Order has been doing that one way or another since 1695. It is one of those organisations whose zeal confers on it a kind of fearlessness. Post-Anschluss, it refused to admit Nazis to its ranks, and was outlawed by Hitler. Hitler's ban expired along with Hitler himself: at the end of World War II, the Americans allowed it to be reinstituted in Europe. By 1966, a certain George Wood had founded its American branch – or in the grander term preferred by the Order, 'chapter'. Today it boasts that it is 'under the Royal Protection of His Majesty Juan Carlos of Spain, the Grand Master Emeritus His Imperial and Royal Highness Archduke Andreas Salvator of Austria and our Grand Master is His Imperial and Royal Highness Istvan von Habsburg Lothringen, Archduke of Austria, Prince of Hungary'.

The weekend would have involved (in no particular order): a fetishizing of guns; an earnest and inadvertently kitsch relationship with European history; an unspoken but dominant note of masculine exclusivity (there are no women members of the Order); lip-service to conservation; and perhaps above all, secrecy, the minor but pervasive thrill of being in on something others are not allowed to witness.

Except the world did end up taking notice. A member of their party retired on the Friday evening, saying he was feeling unwell. He didn't wake up. It would emerge afterwards that he had been experiencing heart problems for some time. His death was perhaps less of a surprise to him than it was to the world's commentariat.

This unfortunate man was Associate Supreme Court Justice Antonin Scalia, one of the most controversial men in America.

A SCALIA-SHAPED VACANCY

Very possibly, if a different right-leaning Supreme Court Justice had died in February, there wouldn't have been quite such emotion behind the weeks and months that followed. Certainly, if a left-leaning judge had passed away, things would have played out very differently.

Scalia – known to his friends as Nino – was the biggest character on the Supreme Court, and along with Chief Justice John Roberts, the most famous justice in America. It was a question of style. During hearings, he could be relied upon to ask the most questions. He tried harder than other judges to escort his colleagues around to his point of view. He wrote the most opinionated opinions – his legal work thrusts you through a legalistic door into the divisiveness of America. These earned a reputation for wit, though in truth they sometimes err on the side of shrillness. Referring to Scalia's fierce thirty-page dissent in *Morrison v. Olson*, Justice Harry Blackman remarked that 'it could be cut down to ten pages if Scalia omitted the screaming'. But Scalia never did – never could – omit the screaming: his life can sometimes read like one primal scream. Real wit is compression, and for Scalia there

Fig 16. Justice Antonin Scalia (1936-2016).[139]

was always more to say – an extra sub-clause of rant, another syllable of rage.

Once again, *The Onion* came close to the mark when news of the death broke: 'Justice Scalia Dead Following 30-Year Battle with Social Progress'. Like so many conservatives today, Scalia really didn't like the America he was seeing: he was avowedly pro-gun, anti marriage equality, a climate change sceptic, and a believer in the 1%: *Citizens United* was classic late-period Scalia. The tone of his public appearances was reliably irritable and cranky. It is noteworthy that as a young man at Georgetown University, he received acclaim as a thespian: Scalia was the kind of zealot who enjoys winding people up with an act. His broadside – 'Get over it' – to those who disagreed with the decision in *Bush v. Gore* was characteristic. If you agreed with him, he was no doubt a hoot. But his appeal was largely dependent on your agreeing with him. Political 'wit' isn't really wit at all: it's just a kind of politics.

But colourful characters leave a gap: he was wonderfully alive. His love of opera, his thrill for legal battle (on the terms he chose to impose on others) and his capacity for friendship, were things for all to mourn, and for his many followers to mourn extravagantly.

Besides, it would be unfair to deny Scalia his place in the history of American jurisprudence. If Scalia was loud, then he was loudly two things: a textualist in statutory interpretation, and a constitutionalist on any matter touching the constitution. They amount more or less to the same thing: Scalia believed that American documents – whether statutes or the Constitution itself – should be interpreted strictly according to their meaning at the time of their drafting. He was opposed to any idea of a 'living constitution', arguing in his dissenting opinion in *Thompson v. Oklahoma* that 'the risk of assessing evolving standards is that it is all too easy to believe that evolution has culminated in one's own views'. This, on the face of it, looks as though it might have the virtues of humility and purity – and a humble, pure judiciary is a good thing if it demarcates judicial power. Legislators draft legislation, but do not rule on it. Judges rule on it, but do not interpret. In practise, though, few judges – and certainly not a judge as political as Scalia – have been able to neuter their own opinions effectively. Scalia, apparently devoted to preserving the original intent of legal documents, is instead the owner of the most idiosyncratic judicial career in American history. Far from blending in to the fabric of American law, he stands out.

Scalia's guiding principles were flawed. Jurisprudence will not be just if humanity is jettisoned in favour of some other rigid principle. Scalia liked strict interpretation of statutes and the Constitution because he knew the country was heading in a more liberal direction, and didn't like it. The framers of dusty statutes and the even dustier Constitution were more likely to agree with him on social issues than anyone living would be. Constitutionalism was a smokescreen for conservatism. His jurisprudence began with the essentially political act of claiming that the world's idea of justice had reached its pinnacle in 1787: his reasoning was extrapolation from an extreme starting-point.

Just as important as the personality of Scalia himself was the balance he left on the Court. Supreme Court justices are nominated by presidents who tend to plump for those with a judicial record in line with their own politics. As politics has become more polarised, the nomination process has become increasingly controversial. Prior to Scalia's death, the Court had tilted to the right by 5-4; contentious decisions had often tended to split in favour of Republicans exactly along those lines.

Now that Scalia had gone, those decisions – and there were many on the upcoming docket including critical cases relating to Obama's immigration executive orders, campaign finance reform and others – would be expected to produce 4-4 results. A locked court would mean that the decision of the lower appellate division would stand. Increasingly, the appeals courts were populated by Democratic judges, which made what followed all the more self-defeating for the Republican Party.

THE REPUBLICAN RESPONSE

After Scalia's death, one assumed there would be a taking stock. It has rarely happened that a Supreme Court Justice has died in a presidential election year, hardly ever that a right-leaning judge has died while a left-leaning President was in office, and arguably never that one so charismatic as Scalia has died at such a comparably tense time.

But the Republican Party does not do restraint. By the Saturday evening, the Senate Majority Leader, Mitch McConnell had already put out the following statement: 'The American people should have a voice in the selection of their next Supreme Court Justice. Therefore, this vacancy should not be filled until we have a new president.'

McConnell's move – crass and too swift – may well prove a political error: polls repeatedly show that the public is tired of this sort of thing. At time of writing, on *RealClearPolitics*, only 13.8% of the public approve of Congress' job performance, and 77% disapprove. If McConnell has read these polls, he appears not to mind them. The White House could not have been surprised: things are now at such a pass in Washington that the surprising move would have been a period of reflection, cooperation with the President's eventual pick, and a swift move to a vote. Meanwhile, the Republican candidates tweeted their responses.

It is often said that you only really know about a presidential candidate when you see them respond to a crisis. Scalia's death turned out to be an interesting microcosm of today's Republican Party. Trump was emotional: 'The totally unexpected loss of Supreme Court Justice Antonin Scalia is a massive setback for the Conservative movement and our COUNTRY!' Cruz was mournful but grimly adamant: 'Justice Scalia was an American hero. We owe it to him, & the Nation, for the Senate to ensure that the next President names his replacement'. Rubio towed the party line in his usual way: 'The next president must nominate a justice who will continue Justice Scalia's unwavering belief in the founding principles'. Bush, deeply Catholic like Scalia, was appropriately respectful at first: 'At Mass, Columba & I prayed for Justice Scalia, who was devout in faith and has been brought home to God in heaven'. Later, in response to Cruz' and Rubio's claims that the seat should be left vacant until 2017, he began to hedge: 'Now it is up to all of us to fight for the principles Justice Scalia espoused and carry forth his legacy'. Kasich was the only one who got it right: 'I am deeply saddened by the passing of Justice Scalia and send my prayers out for his family in this difficult time. His death is a serious loss to our nation and the Court.' He later lamented in a debate, once again the voice of un-listened-to moderation: 'I wish we hadn't rushed so far into politics.'

To take these in turn. The bombast of Trump is concerned to whip up sentiment through adverbs and adjectives that don't need to be there – 'totally' and 'massive', all culminating in the all-caps 'country', which adds nothing besides a non-specific sense of alarm. There is the whiff of Trumpian opportunism – the rage of the writer is synthetic, but he knows he is appealing to a real anger in the audience beyond. Cruz, on the other hand, really is incensed: ideology seeps into everything –even to where it doesn't belong. Bush, Rubio and Kasich must always be responding to a weather he is making: noise in a vapid politics can often be made to look like power. This power is never so great as the ideologue supposes: it has its borders in all reasonable people. But Cruz can often take heart in the response of moderates who want the votes of people who just might, on a bad day, incline towards him. Rubio follows, adopting the same position as Cruz but in apparently centrist language, fooling no-one. Bush, more confident about religious matters than political ones, hedges, and he pleases no one. Kasich opines about the state of things: he knows his own mind, and exhibits some courage in opposing the Cruz orthodoxy, but it is never a sufficiently memorable courage. And how far in the opposite direction does he really go? He is never quite the adult in the room: in a subsequent debate he parroted Cruz and McConnell's calls, and suggested Obama delay a vote, which put him not far from their obstructionist position. And so we have a composite portrait of the modern Republican Party: opportunism and ideology, intellectual frailty, and most importantly, uniting all the candidates, the longing for power.

A BREAK WITH HISTORICAL PRECEDENT?

An irony was at work: Scalia, the great constitutionalist had died, and Republicans, apparently committed to protecting his memory, had become immediately cavalier with the Constitution. Would Scalia have been opposed to the obstructionism done in his name? He was a highly political animal. But he would have had to have been remarkably relaxed about a lifetime's principles in order not to have raised an eyebrow.

The appointments clause of the Constitution reads as follows: The President 'shall nominate, and by and with the Advice and Consent of the Senate, shall appoint [Justices] to the Supreme Court'. The position is clear: upon Scalia's death, the President has two constitutional powers – to nominate and to appoint a replacement with congressional approval. Note that there is no mention that the case should be different in an election year – as Cruz and McConnell claimed. The notion – again a Cruz-McConnell one – that the American people should decide and not the President, conveniently ignores the fact of Obama's re-election in 2012: the American people had made the decision to entrust the presidency, and the carrying out of its duties, to Obama at that time. Unsurprisingly, given this duty, there is no instance of a president not having made a nomination when a position fell vacant on the Court: the Republican Party was shrilly calling for the unprecedented. Of particular interest to the constitutionalist would be – or so one would have thought – the two appointments George Washington made to the Court in 1796, an election year at a time when the Constitution was at least as alive to the protagonists as it is to Ted Cruz today. William Howard Taft, Woodrow Wilson, Herbert Hoover, Franklin D. Roosevelt, and Dwight Eisenhower all successfully made

Supreme Court nominations in election years. It might also be added that Abraham Lincoln made five nominations during the Civil War. The inference is clear: both the Constitution and the historical record suggest that post-Scalia, at the very least, there should have been no controversy about the notion of Obama making a Supreme Court pick.

The Cruz-McConnell camp are able to make some retorts. It is true that no Supreme Court nomination has been made *and* confirmed in an election year since 1932. This is a reflection of how rarely posts fall open on the Court, and in no way alters the position substantively. Besides, Justice Anthony Kennedy, who is still on the bench, was nominated on November 11th 1987, and confirmed on February 3rd 1988 – an election year. Things also went rather choppily in 1968 when President Lyndon Johnson nominated Justice Abe Fortas Chief Justice of the Supreme Court. Fortas would end up withdrawing as the result of a successful filibuster. In that instance, 22 hearings were held, and his eventual withdrawal was the result of ethical breaches he had made while on the Court, and had nothing to do with the fact of its being an election year.[140]

It is true that there are instances – some of them, similarly venerable to the George Washington example – whereby a Senate has voted against a nomination. For instance, in 1795, John Rutledge had made himself so unpopular by denouncing the Jay Treaty with Great Britain that his appointment to the Court was struck down by 14-10. But there again, hearings were held, and a vote allowed. It is also true that there have been instances of Democrats using the filibuster to slow down the process of appointing nominees: President Obama had in fact backed a filibuster against the appointment of one of President Bush's picks Samuel Alito, and after Scalia's death, he expressed his regret for that decision. It hadn't been a constructive approach then, and Obama lamented that, instead of trying to tilt public opinion against Alito, he had instead attempted to 'put sand in the gears'.

The fact remains: by refusing to even allow a vote – and to say that this would be the case even before the President had announced his nominee – the Republican far right had gone into new terrain. Had they kept quiet, left an appropriate amount of time to pass, listened to the nominee, and then voted that eventual nominee down for no reason other than partisan politics, they would still have been acting in an unusual way.

This was no longer about the law; it was about politics. But perhaps there was a certain poetic justice in that – hadn't it always been about politics for Scalia in the first place?

THE MERRICK GARLAND NOMINATION

President Barack Obama faced several considerations in responding to the Republican position.

It was of course an opportunity for him to appoint his third Supreme Court Justice, and therefore tip the balance of the Court in a more liberal direction. 'Legacy' is one of the most overused words in political discourse today, but it would have been in Obama's mind. Presidents rarely get to do anything more important than nominate a judge to the bench: a successful appointment can prevent controversial legislation from being challenged, and set a tone for the country. Obama has always had a mind to firsts when it comes to important positions: for instance, his 2009 pick, Sonia Sotomayor, was the first Supreme Court justice of Latina heritage. Now that the Scalia vacancy had arisen, he would wish to place someone on the Court if at all possible.

However, the virulence of the Republican opposition, together with the fact of its being an election year, had made this no ordinary appointment. Politics would be paramount; the appointment might even affect the result of the election.

The liberal base tends to look for diversity in Supreme Court nominees. It likes landmark appointments, reasoning that the highest court in the land should reflect the heterogeneity of America. One option for Obama was to choose the kind of nominee who might fire up the base, particularly if a vote was refused by the Republicans. Inspiration is, after all, not a quality usually associated with Hillary Clinton. If Obama had been minded to take that approach, then he had some excellent options, most notably Sri Srinivasan, a circuit judge of the United States Court of Appeals for the District of Columbia Circuit. If nominated, Srinivasan would have been the first Indian-American, first Asian-American, and first Hindu candidate for the Supreme Court. It is the sort of appointment any progressive president would have loved to have chalked on the board, and must have been exceptionally tempting for Obama. It would have been made all the more so because Srinivasan had been confirmed into his position by a 97-0 vote: the administration might have been able to ask obstructionist Republicans what had changed between that confirmation and this one. There were other options along these qualified lines. Mariano-Florentino Cuéllar, a justice of the Supreme Court of California, is manifestly qualified, and also considered as a way to inspire the Latino vote. Also highly qualified is Ketanji Brown Jackson, of the District Court of Colombia, who it was speculated might have brought young black women to the polls – a constituency expected to decline with the nation's first black president no longer on the ballot in November.

But President Obama is inherently cautious. As we have seen, his preferred method is to project reasonableness, even if he knows his position will be opposed, thus exposing the flaws in his opponents' arguments. The eventual nomination of the moderate Merrick Garland, the chief judge of the Court of Appeals for the District of Columbia Circuit, must be seen as another example of this tactic.

Merrick Brian Garland was certainly not the kind of judge to get the base excited; the highly successful often have predictable CVs. His career included the usual *magna cum laude* graduation from Harvard, the usual high-flying clerkships in the high courts, the predictable stint at corporate litigation in an exalted firm. There was an attempt to tell a story of against-the-odds success: it was claimed that he had come a long way from the suburbs of Chicago, but no one was likely to be fooled into thinking that Lincolnwood, the happy suburb where he grew up, was any inner-city slum. The facts remained: Garland was white. His judicial record was centrist. He was also old: at 63, it was rather ghoulishly pointed out, his time serving on the bench was likely to be shorter than younger nominees'. He was not a man to excite the liberal base. The standout moment in his career had been his meticulous work as a federal prosecutor on behalf of the Justice Department, in relation to the Oklahoma City bombing in 1995 carried out by Timothy McVeigh and Terry Nichols, which had killed 168 people. One of the many appealing things about Garland is his decision, taken shortly after being made partner of Arnold & Porter, to pursue a career in prosecution in the first place: Garland is not motivated by the dollar. Another appealing feature: Garland is clearly an emotional and decent man. In an interview released by the White House shortly after Garland had been nominated, he teared up at the memory of his father. He fought back tears again when thanking his wife in the Rose Garden. As Obama said when nominating him: 'To find someone with such a long career of public service, marked by complex and sensitive issues; to find someone who just about everyone not only respects, but genuinely likes – that is rare. And

Fig 17. Merrick Garland.[142]

it speaks to who Merrick Garland is – not just as a lawyer, but as a man.'[141] This seems just – America might be teeming and chaotic, but here was a straightforward good man elevated rightfully by hard work to be considered for one of the highest posts in the land.

What was Obama's strategy here? In one sense it had been, surely, to nominate someone above reproach, thereby accentuating in the public's mind the childishness of the Republican Party's leadership. It isn't clear whether Obama really expected Garland to receive a hearing – he must have known from what he had already heard that it would be unlikely. Some felt that Garland was a fall guy, and that Obama, expecting a Democratic victory in the general election, had picked him for political reasons, leaving a more radical pick open for a President Hillary Clinton, should she win. In that scenario, the Republican Party, fearing a highly liberal justice would probably move to confirm Garland in the 'lame duck session' between the election and the inauguration.

But I doubt this. It seems likely that Obama also felt, upon due reflection, that Garland was the best man for the job. As he had done with healthcare, Obama had decided to let the politics take care of themselves.

THE SEPARATION OF POWERS

At the centre of all this controversy is the health or otherwise of a vital idea: the separation of powers. Once again, this idea, so fundamental to the proper functioning of American democracy, began in the Enlightenment.

This time it originated – in its Enlightenment form at least[143]– with the great French philosopher Montesquieu. Some form of hybrid government was probably always intrinsic to the idea of democracy: if more than one person is to hold power, then this state of affairs must be vested somehow in institutions. It had been the case in the Roman Republic – it had been something like the separation of powers which Cicero had sought to defend from the encroaching ambition of first one Caesar, then another. Montesquieu's contribution was to firmly delineate the tripartite system: power should be spread among the judiciary, the executive, and the legislature. John Locke also endorsed the idea. The tripartite system was also uppermost in the minds of the Founding Fathers when they came in that hot, fly-ridden summer of 1787 to draft the Constitution of the United States. James Madison – later to become the nation's fourth president, and a precocious 36-year-old in the realm of political theory if ever there was one – explained the idea behind a checks and balances system: if people 'were angels, no government would be necessary'.[144] Those who drafted the constitution were mindful of the possible abuse that can come from human sinfulness. High-minded, embarked on a great enterprise, they made no provision for 21st century partisan childishness.

'The Founding Fathers' is a phrase uttered with a certain reverence by Americans; one can sometimes forget how divided those fathers were. Alexander Hamilton, the first US Secretary of the Treasury, considered the people 'a great beast', whereas George Mason, one of the authors of the Virginia Declaration of Rights, spoke of the need to set free 'the genius of the people'. The American system is a fudge of this argument, along the lines of a divided legislature. The House of Representatives is elected every two years: this was intended to be 'the grand repository of the democratic principle of the Government' (Mason again). However, each senator, to appease the Hamiltonians, only condescends to face the electorate every six years – though these elections are staggered so that every two years approximately one third of senate seats is up for grabs. The US system therefore mingles the wish to give the people their say with a strong dose of doubt as to whether anyone will much like what they are saying. This fundamental doubt as to whether a human being can be trusted can be seen in the way the presidency was shaped. The president's power is limited both in terms of declaring war and in the processes of impeachment: thus was Richard Nixon doomed as early as 1787. However the president, though potentially fallible, is also a check on the legislature – from which we get the presidential veto. But by far the least contentious of the three branches in 1787 – and until now, ever since – has been the judiciary. It might be said that those drafting the laws of America could have foreseen a demagogue more or less in the Trump mould, but not a highly politicised judge like Scalia. True, there was an implied right to judicial review of legislation all along, and this right could always have been open to abuse. But the law can make a virtue of dryness, and what is most noticeable about discussions surrounding the founding of the country is how little they discussed the judiciary compared to the other branches. They were ultimately inclined to be optimistic: out of all this back and forth, the will of the people – in the minds of men like Madison and Mason, a sort of mystical revered thing – would rise up, and justice would reign.

To an enormous extent, it has worked. Richard Nixon abused his executive power and would have been impeached had he not resigned. Unpopular officials are regularly voted out. It can be called messy – or as Obama might put it, not yet 'perfected' – but it is broadly functional. What those who drafted the Constitution did not foresee was, of course, modern politics – that the national debate would become so compressed by 21st century forms of media that senators and congressmen, ostensibly there to represent the interests of their locality, could be bullied into voting against their consciences by a national campaign leveraged against them. Nor did they foresee the modern party system and its intensely partisan nature, whereby a party apparatus will seek to impose a unanimous position of obstruction, thereby grinding government to a halt. Politics at the time of drafting the Constitution was comparatively localised and civic; today it is too often a vehicle for whipped-up emotion. Today's

congressman is the victim of national cross-
currents, and more likely to be a careerist.

America was founded by philosophers
who expected those in government to look to the
overall health of their country. They had good
reasons for doing so – they had just fought a
major war of independence, and there was no
guarantee that the rest of the world would leave
them alone. Today, in its military might, with
survival assured, and – notwithstanding the rise
of China – supremacy more or less ongoing, a
new kind of petty-minded decision-making has
entered America's bloodstream.

AFTER THE GARLAND NOMINATION

It became clear over time that the White House
was winning the war of public opinion.

The Garland pick may not have fired up
too many liberals, but it was broadly popular.
An NBC-Wall Street Poll asked respondents in
February, shortly after Scalia's death, whether
President Obama should appoint a new justice
to the Court or whether the position should be
left vacant. The vote split along partisan lines:
43% said a vote should take place; 42% said it

should be left vacant until after the election; 15% said that they didn't have an opinion. By April, the same organisation reported a shift in opinion when the question was asked: 52% now thought a vote should take place, only 30% thought the seat should be left vacant, and 18% now had no opinion.[145] Interestingly, many of these gains were among Republicans, suggesting that perhaps even traditional G.O.P. voters were growing tired of some of their party's shenanigans – or at least had begun to realise that they might prove electorally damaging. Meanwhile, the Constitutional Responsibility Project – which is campaigning for the Garland nomination – published a report indicating that some 1.5 million petition signatures have been sent to Congress in support of the Obama administration's pick. Some Republican senators in swing states have therefore been cornered into meeting with Garland. Pennsylvania Senator Pat Toomey said that he would conduct a meeting 'out of respect for both the president and the judge'. Senator Susan Collins of Maine went one further and called for hearings. Mark Kirk of Illinois did the same.

Will this controversy affect the outcome of the presidential election? It is unlikely that it helps the Republicans. Pettiness is rarely good politics. On the other hand, there will be many issues at stake, and already by May, the Garland nomination was beginning to be side-lined by the press. After the Trump nomination, opinion polls began to show liberals wavering: a Clinton win might open the door to a nomination more in line with liberal priorities – a Srinivasan for example.

However things pan out, it is another indication of the importance of this election that even the justice system is no longer immune to the effects of political obstructionism and deadlock. The partisan media is like the flood in the Pushkin poem 'The Bronze Horseman', which upturns the social order, until what you were beforehand doesn't matter: it only matters whether you can swim. A.J.P. Taylor attributed the rise of Hitler in part to the presence of amateurs at the very top. Amateurism is unhappy until it has taken professionalism down a peg or two. Merrick Garland, in his modesty and even in his uninterestingness, stands for a way of doing things which lies in that blessed realm beyond Fox News and CNN, where what matters isn't the news cycle, but the complex detail of a given problem: it is the country of the

Enlightenment, and it is sunny there.

Even if Obama had been able to nominate the ghost of Scalia himself, one suspects that the words would have been hardly out of Cruz' mouth before he himself could have deciphered their meaning: 'No.'

CHAPTER TEN – THE FUTURE OF THE ENLIGHTENMENT

The scientific approach to the examination of phenomena is a defence against the pure emotion of fear.

–Tom Stoppard, *Rosencrantz and Guildenstern are Dead*

A brief digression about William Shakespeare. In *Hamlet,* Marcellus observes that 'something is rotten in the state of Denmark'. In *Othello*, Othello himself predicts that, when he can no longer love Desdemona, 'chaos is come again'. Shakespeare's tragedies show the superb variety of life – one might say they teem with a freedom which equates with one's best idea of America – but they also excel at showing the breakdown of systems as triggered by the character flaws of elevated men and women. Shakespeare understood that kingships and dukedoms are particularly vulnerable to the fragile psyche of the individual. In that sense, his plays might be said to open up onto democracy – though not even he could ever have imagined such a crazy thing as a US presidential primary. Even so, democracy works by spreading this

Shakespearean risk. All our individual fragilities
– Anthony's hedonism, or Macbeth's ambition
– our quirks and blind spots, mismanagements
and griefs are pooled together with whatever
we can muster of common sense or insight,
our good moments, and better angels. At
election time, the pot is stirred in the hope that
a medicine of reasonableness shall emerge:
democracy is our remedy against ourselves.

The hope is that the country which has
chosen democracy moves down the years, not
along a series of King Lear- or Hamlet-style
crack-ups, where every individual hurt or scheme
ripples miserably through the state, but slowly,
even with a certain dullness, toward the next
generation. The first kind of system, built around
kings and their vulnerabilities, gives us our
epic poetry, our Homer and Virgil, *Beowulf* and
Shakespeare. Democracy bequeaths instead
a story in prose; the novel rose up as the only
form able to accommodate the liberation of
teeming multitudes. Ideas are shared; scientific
progress is made. Piecemeal, but discernibly,
the standard of living rises. Most countries given
the chance – including America – have deemed
this worth a shot.

THE TROUBLE WITH DEMOCRACY

That's how it's meant to go, and as we have
seen, America has gone broadly that way. This
is the America many of us love, and revel in
– the one we look forward to visiting. It is the
America I spoke of in Chapter Two – a country
which is kind, witty and endlessly innovative.
It is a place of sophistication and cheer, which
gives rise to lives we admire – or, to try another
list, where the satires of Joseph Heller and
Mark Twain complement the wistful wisdom of
Marilynne Robinson; where the splurge of the
Jackson Pollock canvas is shown next to the
eerie works of Mark Rothko; where Einstein and
Bohr have come to argue about the Theory of
Everything; where *Death of a Salesman* is staged
one night, and Louis C.K. might be on the next.
It is a place of untrammelled opportunity and
even magnificence, a country that the Founding
Fathers, quintessential Enlightenment figures
like Thomas Jefferson and Benjamin Franklin,
would have delighted in.

But this book shows glimmers of another
story, a rarer one. It's rarer because for most
people, it proves a very bad option. We know
it happens from time to time in history, but it's

difficult to say how it does happen. All we know is that sometimes the subjects of a democracy become alienated *en masse* from the democratic process. It can be to do with fluctuations in national strength – or fluctuations in mass *perception* of national strength – and the fear and exclusion that comes from that. These things are always present in some degree, even in stable systems. But in the instances I am describing, fear sharpens, and exclusion causes rage. Most importantly, someone comes along who articulates – but also takes advantage of – these extreme emotions. *Build a wall. Ban the Muslims. Cut the government. It's a revolution.*

There are weaknesses in the democratic process that make this possible – chinks in its armour. How empowering, after all, is a vote for president? It happens once every four years, and the nuance of your opinion, all the things you think and feel about the world, are not incorporated. Many Americans in 2016 appear to have looked at the system and thought just like Rhett Benhoff, whom we met briefly in Chapter Eight: I am not getting a fair shake. Their vote has become unusually emotional. Democratic systems, designed to be complex, sometimes give to a sufficiently large majority of their subjects the impression not so much of a glorious symphony, but of something cacophonous and intractable.

All this will have a neuroscientific explanation. We are not too far from establishing the beginnings of a scientific basis for what happens at election time. The psychologist Joshua Greene is able to point to the part of the brain that deals with emotional responses (the amygdala) and those which flesh out a more reasoned response to data (the parietal lobe): the former is sometimes more dominant than one would like. Karen Stenner's classic study *The Authoritarian Dynamic* put forward the theory, simple on the face of it, but with potentially devastating implications, that some people are simply predisposed to seek authoritarian solutions when they believe that their security is under threat. Jonathan Haidt described this response mechanism: 'In case of moral threat, lock down the borders, kick out those who are different, and punish those who are morally deviant.'[146] Elections might be deemed a spectacle of millions of neurons firing. Sometimes they fire into calm: for instance, we tell the pollster on the phone that Merrick Garland should be allowed an up-and-down vote. At other times they light up, and their owner goes out and buys a Donald Trump hat. As often with political science, one is never quite sure how ground-breaking this research is in real terms, since we already know these things are happening.

Without the burden of needing to prove anything scientifically, it is possible to speculate further: we needn't think only in terms of authoritarianism. One neuron one would particularly expect to be firing among Trump supporters is the one reporting how miserable it is to be confused. We all know the feeling of vexation we have when we come up against a problem, emotional or intellectual, which we cannot grasp. For this author it has always been mathematics: during the writing of this book, I have wondered what it would be like to inhabit a world where the frustration of not being able to manage, say, simple algebra had migrated into other areas of life, into one's entire sense of self. It is then, when confusion has become the dominant mode, that radical and radically simplifying solutions, like those touted by Cruz or Trump might be appealing.

THE SPECTRE OF COMPLEXITY

In 2016, confusion is everywhere. To return briefly
to Shakespeare, the words spoken by Macduff
in *Macbeth* have often come to mind when
writing this book: 'Confusion now hath made its
masterpiece'.

How do confusion and fear play out
in politics? This time around, something like
the following appears to have happened: a
pragmatic sort like Obama is elected President.
He proceeds to apply evidence-based solutions
to certain problems identified during the
campaign, and to those which subsequently land
on his desk. Some good is done, but the mess
of the world persists. Politicians are continually
rubbing up against the complexity of the world.
In a sense, our disappointment is odd. Did we
really expect every problem to go away because
of one man's elevation to the presidency? Are
we annoyed to have been duped into taking part
in the process itself, the same way one may feel
fairly exhausted after spending an afternoon
screaming at a football match when our team
didn't win?

Or are we simply exasperated by the
problems themselves?

For simplicity's sake, one would like to say that the rage in America today has to do with these defeated expectations. All governments exist in postlapsarian worlds: election day is eating the apple. This was especially true of Obama's administration, for which hopes were so high to begin with. Under that analysis, presidents are to some extent always victims of the process that put them in the presidency. The extraordinarius ends up all too human. Modern elections, which might consist of concerted attempts to look at problems, function instead as a radical suspension from them: they have become bogus exercises in simplification. Talk of Hope or Change cedes, for instance, to horse-trading to get healthcare passed, or the undelightful but necessary process of setting up the Consumer Financial Protection Bureau. The Trump voter's rage lurks in the dull meeting he – it's usually a 'he' – didn't attend, and probably would have found crushingly dull if he had.

And yet our feelings about politics aren't only about process: everything keeps coming back to our lives. If the political process were merely a self-contained entertainment, politics would exist, roughly where Donald Trump would like it to exist, within the realm of televisual fantasy. The issues governments face are highly complex – perhaps insolubly so. They need to be articulated in a political language, then fixed in primarily financial terms. Contemporary politicians are increasingly beholden to economists. It used to be the other way round: there is now no king checking in with his chancellery as a formality to confirm that taxes could be raised to fund that overseas jaunt which, apropos of not much, just popped into his mind. Instead, the banks come to presidents and tell them, one hopes a little sheepishly, about the economy they just screwed up while everyone was out on the election trail. Economists are not always, as the Great Recession shows, completely sure what is going on. Much of the time, we are driving blindfolded.

Even from the president's side of the desk, where we would hope to find wisdom, the complexity of the world makes decision-making difficult. Politicians campaign on certainties and slogans that will have limited application to the minutiae of events. Leaders would never publicly concede the point, but they run up daily against the limits of the Enlightenment. A good example of this phenomenon in recent years is Obama's decision to order the mission against Osama bin

Laden in May 2011: after exhaustive analysis of the compound in Abbottabad and much weighing of risk, Obama summed up the evidence: 'This is 50-50'. The Enlightenment isn't an absolute stick to wield against problems. Politics will often come down to the moral character of the decision-maker, even to hunch: Napoleon famously prized a lucky general above all else. All politicians are improvisers, but they come to public attention first as prophets.

Even so the Bush administration is a case study around what can happen when the analytical frame of mind becomes distrusted.

A Trump presidency would be a dangerous case study in what would happen if it were hardly used at all.

THE SIZE OF THE STATE

The 2016 election shows a variegated revolt against the complicated nature of the world. In earlier chapters, I have shown that that system is under strain, since for many Americans the main parties seem to be imperfectly representing their interests, or not representing them at all.

But I have been skirting around another important point about 2016: the right-wing view of life is traditionally a vital part of any democracy. It may not always feel like it in 2016, but we want a healthy Republican Party. The novels of Franz Kafka remind us that when a system is too labyrinthine to understand, it is also infinitely open to abuse: at their best, Republicans would simply wish to reduce the complexity of unwarranted government, and make lives more streamlined. It is vital that every democracy has a party that can watch out for the sort of agglomeration of faceless power which Charles Dickens brilliantly satirised in *Little Dorrit* (1855-7):

> The Circumlocution Office was (as everybody knows without being told) the most important Department under Government. No public business of any kind could possibly be done at any time without the acquiescence of the Circumlocution Office. Its finger was in the largest public pie, and in the smallest public tart. It was equally impossible to do the plainest right and to undo the plainest wrong without the

express authority of the Circumlocution Office. If another Gunpowder Plot had been discovered half an hour before the lighting of the match, nobody would have been justified in saving the parliament until there had been half a score of boards, half a bushel of minutes, several sacks of official memoranda, and a family-vault full of ungrammatical correspondence, on the part of the Circumlocution Office.[147]

This urgent need to question the size of government resurfaces in another great novelist of our own time. In *Diary of a Bad Year* (2007), J.M. Coetzee is especially concerned with the state, and in particular the way in which we all inherit certain obligations towards it, conceded by the previous generation without our say-so. In *The Social Contract* Rousseau famously wrote: 'Man is born free but everywhere he is in chains'. But Rousseau's philosophy contributed to a system which leaves those chains intact: it's only that the ownership of them has passed from a king to a parliament. And parliament usually means some government minister or other – i.e. someone who has a distinct resemblance to a king. Here is Coetzee:

> To regain touch, you must at every
> moment remind yourself of what it is like
> to come face to face with the state—the
> democratic state or any other—in the
> person of the state official. Then ask
> yourself: Who serves whom? Who is the
> servant, who the master?[148]

When queuing in our law courts, or when
experiencing our annual run-ins with HMRC,
we have all wondered as much, and it will
always be an important check to have parties
in democracies whose tendency is to query
whether government, in any given instance,
needs to be there, and whether it is actually
working.

If America were to lose a party
intelligently arguing that position, it would have
lost much, even if the position can be open to
the abuses of oversimplification – as in the
campaign of Ted Cruz. It can sometimes seem
that the real danger of Donald Trump isn't that
he might defeat Hillary Clinton in the general
election, but that he defeated John Kasich in the
primary.

NOTES TOWARDS A SYNTHESIS

The leftist view of life is, in a different way, a response to the complexity of life. Like the right wing view, it is not without problems. This was vividly illustrated to President Obama when he first took office, when then Defence Secretary Robert Gates said to him: 'Mr President, one thing I can guarantee you is that at this moment, somewhere, somehow, somebody in the federal government is screwing up.' It was a sobering confrontation with the unwieldy nature of government delivered by a moderate Republican to a moderate Democrat. The meaning was not lost on Obama, who has always emphasised, as he did in his first inaugural, the importance of government working properly.

In general, the left-leaning mind sees a world of screw-up and chaos which needs to be kept in check – the instinct to legislate at problems is deeply embedded. This is usually a preferable alternative to doing nothing, but it might be that on occasion these good instincts can lead, in time, to the Circumlocution Office. Somewhere beyond these debates is the notion that civilisation neighbours an appalling nature. This state of affairs was articulated in the famous passage in Hobbes' *Leviathan*:

In such condition [ie in the natural human condition without the State] there is no place for industry, because the fruit thereof is uncertain, and consequently, no culture of the earth, no navigation, nor the use of commodities that may be imported by sea, no commodious building, no instruments of moving and removing such things as require much force, no knowledge of the face of the earth, no account of time, no arts, no letters, no society, and which is worst of all, continual fear and danger of violent death, and the life of man, solitary, poor, nasty, brutish, and short.[149]

Hobbes felt that humankind, labouring under such a predicament would therefore naturally agree to submit to government in a bid to make life less poor, less nasty, less brutish, and somewhat longer. His emphasis was on the total nature of that submission. Locke, as we saw in Chapter One, thought humankind somewhat pluckier: subjects could at least demand their consent.

Both interpretations of what to do about this somewhat regrettable state of affairs – right and left – could be called pessimistic. Liberals see that natural Hobbesian state as perilously close – in effect, we are always on the brink and must act to stave off a return to the dark ages. Conservatives don't trust the people above them to make systems which are sufficiently humane or helpful to really make things any better. Both are open to caricature. In a recent article in *The National Review,* 'Our Hobbesian Left', Kevin Williamson summarised the liberal position:

> Argue for a reduction in taxes, or a more restrictive interpretation of delegated powers, or allowing the states to take the lead on health care and education, and they're sure that the next step is a Hobbesian hootenanny in which all of our rump roasts are crawling with bacteria, somebody snatches Piggy's glasses, and, worst of all, there's no NPR [National Public Radio] to ask what it all means.[150]

Similarly, although the 2016 right isn't always susceptible of caricature, having gone so far in that direction themselves, there is such a thing as the liberal who can go too far in characterising all those on the right as hard-hearted, gun-toting financiers who oppose all social progress.

This is another example of how readily political discourse turns to cliché – cliché, that other popular response to the fact that the world is complicated. There is always the suspicion that these two opposing views don't quite answer to reality. Each is too simplistic. Throughout his presidency, Obama has repeatedly drawn attention to the possibility of a middle-ground. Put simply, there are two things that are easy to imagine which answer neither the 'right' nor the 'left' view of life – namely, a so-called 'liberal' who thinks a given government program doesn't work, and a 'conservative' who thinks a given government program does.

But in such instances are the labels 'liberal' or 'conservative' really of much use? To the extent that the answer is no, there is tension in the two-party system.

WHAT NEXT?

With economic headwinds from China, potential fragmentation in the European Union, the Iran nuclear deal still febrile, and worries about the planet's future uppermost in the minds of many, it feels a dangerous time for America to be trying out the following experiment: What happens when one party in the two-party system of the most powerful country on earth takes leave of its senses?

What kind of election will 2016's be? To an unprecedented degree, it will involve mud-slinging by Trump. Bill Clinton's sex life will be discussed, along with Hillary's response to it. One cannot definitely say that violence will erupt regularly at Trump rally venues as they have so far, but unlike any election in recent history, one cannot definitely say that the ground note of the elections won't be threat, rage and tantrum.

And the result? That will hinge on the question: how effectively can Trump tack to the centre? On the one hand, it looks a tall order. His hostile takeover of the Republican Party betrayed one of the cardinal rules of presidential campaigns. You need to win your nomination with minimal fuss, and without going too far to the fringes of your own party. Gore Vidal called the country the United States of Amnesia with good reason: the primary candidate counts on few people having paid attention until the general election season, whereupon centrist positions can be adopted with the least pain. Trump has broken this rule to an outrageous extent. He cannot unsay what he has said about the wall with Mexico, the crass characterisations he has perpetrated about women, his uncertain reaction to the endorsement of former Ku Klux Klan Grand Wizard David Duke, nor his advocacy of torture, and his mockery of the disabled. These things were nothing if not memorable. He has perpetrated an anti-minorities campaign in an America where minorities are on the rise.

For this reason, the expectation among many commentators is that Trump will lose, and ordinary business will resume in 2020. In that year, a moderate candidate, a resurgent Rubio, perhaps – one who has learned the courage of his own convictions, or found some – might win the Republican nomination, tack to the centre ground, and then face a straight fight with a Hillary Clinton seeking re-election. Such a candidate might be assisted in a curious way by Obama's absence: under Bush, the party showed signs that it had the capacity to move towards a more tolerant view of the Muslim world. It was President Bush, after all, who visited the Baltimore mosque six days after September 11 to describe Islam as a religion of peace. Of course, Bush's ensuing policies did very little for world peace. But if the Republican leadership could rediscover that note of tolerance – and perhaps harmonize it with Trump's cathartic admission that the War on Iraq was a mistake – then it would instantly render itself more electable. One suspects that Hillary Clinton would struggle to win a fourth term in elected office against even a moderately appealing centre-right candidate: it is the natural pendulum of politics.

But this year has also taught us not to be cavalier with predictions: it has been the year of 'perhaps', 'might' and 'maybe'. The trouble with the idea of a 2020 moderate candidate is that it would be some U-turn for a party deeply entrenched in radicalism, both at the state and at the federal level. The question then arises: how much does reality insist on itself for human beings? How much rage will America permit itself about routine economic ups-and-downs and the always difficult Middle East? It is not completely clear that another defeat at the presidential level would chasten a huge chunk of the G.O.P. Under that analysis, the Republican Party might refuse to move to the centre and prove terminally unelectable at the presidential level. In this prediction, the Democratic Party would buck the current trend of presidential politics in the two-party system and win not just a third straight election in 2016, but also a fourth in 2020. At what point would electoral punishment spawn a Republican nominee for the presidency who, say, accepted the science on climate change? Would it be forced to drift back into the mainstream of political argument, tamp down its rhetoric, and eventually win the presidency again under a centre-right candidate in the mould of George H.W. Bush? Perhaps the fever would break. Perhaps presidents would be able to legislate again.

But if the Republican Party didn't change, the country would start to look like an especially ineffective one-party system with Democrats returning for the foreseeable future at the presidential level when people are paying attention, but Republicans winning a kind of eternal protest vote in mid-term elections. America would be tarred for the long-term by an entirely rancorous politics: major legislation would be a thing of the past, and the president – always a Democrat – would be forced to govern primarily by executive order (as Obama has done for six years now). This interpretation feels too static to be true: it is unlikely that the country will step into the same river twice, then a third time, then a fourth. But it is the pattern of the last election, and perhaps this one, so neither is it impossible.

OR CHAOS

Hovering over this book has been the spectre of Nazi Germany – the most vivid image we have of what happens when a country that looks civilised permits fear to govern its discourse, then gives way to violent ideology.

One is hopeful that America will not go down this route. For all its difficulties, it is still a country with declining unemployment, which now has an improved healthcare system, greater tolerance in many quarters, and a less wasteful foreign policy. Nothing so cataclysmic as defeat in the First World War nor anything so dramatic as Weimar-era hyperinflation has befallen it. This optimism must, alas, be tempered with caution. Part of the reason one can't be certain America will remain a moderate country is that we don't have much experience of how civilised countries veer toward extremism: it has happened with gratifying rarity. But this description by Gibbon at the end of *The Decline and Fall of the Roman Empire* strikes too many chords with modern America for me not to quote it:

> A long period of distress and anarchy, in which empire, and arts, and riches, had migrated from the banks of the Tiber, was incapable of restoring or adorning the city; and, as all that is human must retrograde if it do not advance, every successive age must have hastened the ruin of the works of antiquity.[151]

'Must retrograde if it do not advance' – it is an image of stagnation. *Something is rotten in the state of Denmark*. During the Obama years, bills have been produced by Congress in the certain knowledge that they would be vetoed by the President. In 2016, the President produced a budget and Congress refused even to look at it. There is a torpor in all this that is worrying. It is this deadlock which Trump and Cruz promise to remove. Stagnation sometimes feels built into the system: the Founding Fathers were operating at the fringes of a vast stillness, which was also a gigantic possibility: America. They feared a corrupt state, not an uncompetitive one. Nor could they imagine the pace of modern progress, and the need for agility in policy-making to legislate against a turbulent reality.

There has been another leitmotif to this book: we have never had a lurch toward extremism at a time when the planet was also, according to the vast majority of scientific opinion, under threat. America is the world's second largest polluter. It has just – with great difficulty – secured the bilateral agreement (mentioned in Chapter Four) with China, the world's largest. All Obama's moves on climate change, significant though they are, remain both insufficient and fragile, and could easily be undone by future presidents. There remains the fear that, in climate change, humankind has been presented with a problem which it will be unable to solve, not because it was really insoluble, but because a small tranche of modern America was unwilling to accept it as a problem. Even in the unlikely event that the scientific community turns out to have been wrong, or engaged in some shadowy project of unprecedented alarmism, one would still feel that the Republicans should have looked upon the allegations with an open mind: even Ted Cruz would surely have to admit that he is physical, and therefore subject to climate.

So to return to where I began – to W.H. Auden in 1939 in that New York café. Earlier in that year, he had written his great eulogy 'In Memory of W.B. Yeats', in which he had written the line: 'Poetry makes nothing happen'. It remains true: speculation dances around reality – in 2016 again, we all of us must wait and see. But Auden had also ended that poem in memory of Yeats with a plea one wants to send across the seas – which most probably *are* rising – like a message in a bottle, for as many Americans as possible to read:

> In the deserts of the heart
> Let the healing fountain start,
> In the prison of his days
> Teach the free man how to praise.

It is the hope of this book that the free man is usually inclined to praise, among other things, his free condition – freedom which has always meant, in one way or another, tolerance of your neighbour.

In watching the process unfold, I find myself in wonder at the mess and passion of democracy, and fascinated by its vulnerability, as one might be fascinated by any beautiful, fragile thing. 319 million people are about to make the deliberations which affect the rest of us so much. The suspicion remains that the best person for the job is already in there and barred from running again. There is the sense that the 20th of January, 2017 – the day the next president will be sworn in – cannot be a wholly good one. One simply, to use one of the incumbent's favourite words, hopes it isn't a very bad one.

ACKNOWLEDGEMENTS

I want to thank my publisher Todd Swift for giving me the opportunity to write this book: it would not exist if not for his generosity, energy and creativity. In the Squint series, he seems to me to have helped bring about, in a matter of a few months, a renaissance in the book-length political essay – no small achievement, and in his constant championing of new writers, also a selfless one. I also want to thank Kelly Davio for her enthusiastic and thorough work on the book. She has brought to the editing process not only an invaluable American perspective on this election, but also her poet's sensibility with language: I am grateful for both.

I also want to thank my parents Gordon and Sue Jackson for their constant support and kindness. This book is dedicated particularly to my father in his mayoral year. Over many Sunday lunches, we have talked politics, and I always enjoy learning his perspective. In his tireless work for his locality, he has helped me to understand that although it might be easier on the face of it to fix a fence than to persuade a bank to fix an economy, without people mending fences, you might never have arrived at the nation state in the first place. I am grateful for his love, inspiration and support.

Lastly I want to thank my wife Jade who has been as supportive today, 39 weeks into her pregnancy, as she was at 24 weeks when I began sketching out this book. She has never yet complained about being forced to watch hours of Donald Trump on CNN, and has even been instrumental in helping me research the US criminal justice system by accompanying me in back-to-back episodes of *The Mentalist*. Books about politics are really about the future, and I can already guess that the only timeline that matters to parents is the timeline their children will see. That has made this short book not just a privilege, but also in its small way, a duty – and for me, the first of its kind.

C.J – 27th May 2016

ENDNOTES

0 Euripides, Alcestis and Other Plays, trans. P. Vellacott, Penguin Classics (1953), p. 63.

1 M. Willstein, 'Ricky Gervais: Don't Worry, "Nothing Will Happen" If Trump Is Elected President', published in *The Daily Beast*, 7th May 2016.

2 Remarks made by President Barack Obama at a joint press conference with Prime Minister David Cameron on 22nd April 2016.

3 B. Johnson, 'UK and America can be better friends than ever Mr Obama... if we LEAVE the EU', published in *The Sun*, 23rd April 2016. Johnson didn't mention that Obama had understandably replaced the Churchill bust with one of Martin Luther King Jr.

4 J. Freedland, 'It took Barack Obama to crush the Brexit fantasy,' published in *The Guardian*, 22nd April 2016.

5 W. Shakespeare, *Anthony and Cleopatra*, Act V, Scene 1, 34-35, Oxford Second Edition, p.1025.

6 *http://www.ukpolitical.info/Expenditure.htm*.

7 *http://elections.nytimes.com/2012/campaign-finance*.

8 Albert R. Hunt, How Record Spending Will Affect the Election, published in *Bloomberg View*, 26th April 2015.

9 Thucydides, *History of the Peloponnesian War,* Book II, 37 In the Penguin Classics 1972 revised edition (translated by R. Warner with an introduction and notes by M.I. Finley). The relevant section can be found on page 145.

10 This work is in the public domain in its country of origin and other countries and areas where the copyright term is the author's life plus 100 years or less. The work of art depicted in this image

and the reproduction thereof are in the public domain worldwide. The reproduction is part of a collection of reproductions compiled by The Yorck Project. The compilation copyright is held by Zenodot Verlagsgesellschaft mbH and licensed under the GNU Free Documentation License.

11 This image was originally posted to Flickr by nathanmac87 at https://flickr.com/photos/72841285@N00/25619534911. It was reviewed on 12 March 2016 by the FlickreviewR robot and was confirmed to be licensed under the terms of the cc-by-2.0. This file is therefore licensed under the Creative Commons Attribution 2.0 Generic license. https://creativecommons.org/licenses/by/2.0/legalcode

12 From W.H. Auden, September 1,1939. This poem is of course regularly anthologised but can be found on page 245 of *The English Auden*, published by Faber and Faber, ed. E. Mendelson, 1977.

13 Like so many of Vidal's best remarks this is now so widely quoted as to be difficult to track down. It appeared originally in an essay called 'Gods and Greens', which is collected in *A View from the Diner's Club*, Andre Deutsch, 1991, but also appears often in articles about Vidal, including 'Gore Vidal: 26 of the Best' published in *The Guardian*, 1st August 2012.

14 D. Trump statement on preventing Muslim immigration, December 7th 2015.

15 Franklin Delano Roosevelt, Madison Square Garden speech, October 31st, 1936.

16 P. Roth, *The Plot Against America*, Houghton Mifflin Harcourt, 2004, p. 1.

17 F. Bacon, *The New Organon: or True Directions Concerning the Interpretation of Nature*, 1620 published in J.M Robertson, *The Philosophical Works of Francis Bacon*, p. 281, George Routledge and Sons, 1905.

18 C. Nicholl, Leonardo da Vinci, *The Flights of the Mind*, Penguin

Books, 2004, p. 12.

19 Quoted in 'Christopher Hitchens in Quotes', published in *The Telegraph*, 16th December 2011.

20 C. James, 'From Log Cabin to Log Cabin', published in *The New Statesman*, 1978.

21 M. Amis, 'Ronald Reagan', first published in *The Sunday Telegraph* in 1979, then collected in *The Moronic Inferno and Other Visits to America*, 1986, p. 89.

22 In a recent book by the Shakespearean scholar Stephen Greenblatt, *Shakespeare's Freedom* (University of Chicago Press, 2010), Greenblatt tells of an occasion at the White House at the height of the Lewinsky affair. Greenblatt reports himself as asking Clinton a trifle provocatively: 'Mr President, don't you think that *Macbeth* is a great play about an immensely ambitious man who feels compelled to do things that he knows are politically and morally disastrous?' Clinton replied: 'I think Macbeth is a great play about someone whose immense ambition has an ethically inadequate object.' Impressed, Greenblatt concluded that Clinton had missed his vocation. The anecdote can be found on page 74.

23 Quoted in K. Gormley, *The Death of American Virtue: Clinton v. Starr*, Crown Publishers, 2010, pp. 89-90.

24 K. Rove, 'Bush is A Book Lover', *The Wall Street Journal*, December 26th, 2008.

25 There is an excellent analysis of the strange marriage of convenience between Trump and Palin in O. Jones, *Donald Trump: The Rhetoric*, Squint, 2016, pp. 69-74.

26 Remarks by Sarah Palin to Dr. James Dobson on *Focus in the Family*, October 22nd 2008.

27 There is also the possibility that as a result of the Trump nomination, McCain may lose his senate seat in 2016. Arizona

is now perceived as an area of particular weakness for the Republicans as the result of Trump's anti-immigration policies: the state is over 30% Latino.

28 Under Creative Commons Attribution 2.0 Generic license. Attribution: Count to Ten. https://creativecommons.org/licenses/by/2.0/legalcode

29 'Obama Says First Lady Told Him She Might Want a Gun — Depending on Where They Lived', published in *Time*, January 7th 2016.

30 M. Grunwald, 'The Party of No', published in *Time*, 23rd August 2012.

31 'When did McConnell say he wanted to make Obama a one-term President?' published in *The Washington Post*, 24th September, 2012.

32 G.W. Bush, *Decision Points*, Random House, 2010, p. 459.

33 P. Krugman, 'The Making of A Mess,' published in *The New York Times*, 3rd December, 2007.

34 Financial Crisis Enquiry Commission Report, January 27th 2011.

35 The decision to do so was plainly a temperamental one. Obama clearly found in Bernanke a kindred spirit. He later praised him for his calm.

36 This image or file is a work of a U.S. Air Force Airman or employee, taken or made as part of that person's official duties. As a work of the U.S. federal government, the image or file is in the public domain in the United States. Taken by: Master Sgt. Cecilio Ricardo, U.S. Air Force.

37 This image is under Creative Commons License 3.0. Author David Shankbone.

38 M. Grunwald, 'The Nation He Built', published in *Politico*, January 7th 2016.

39 Basically, a system whereby most individuals are required to pay for their own coverage, or face a penalty. No-one likes paying for this sort of thing, which is why the eventual Obamacare legislation (see Chapter Four) has the word 'affordable' so prominently in its title.

40 He also didn't expect to be putting forward an individual mandate-based plan himself. Until at least the middle of 2009 he had hoped for a more radical plan (See Chapter Four).

41 Quoted in J. McCormick, Chicago Tribune, published on September 21st 2007.

42 D. Rumsfeld, US Department of Defense Press Briefing, February 12, 2002.

43 J. Robertson, *Iraq: A History*, One World Publications, 2015, p. 324.

44 This image is a work of a U.S. military or Department of Defense employee, taken or made as part of that person›s official duties. As a work of the U.S. federal government, the image is in the public domain. Author: United States Armed Forces.

45 This image is a work of a U.S. military or Department of Defense employee, taken or made as part of that person's official duties. As a work of the U.S. federal government, the image is in the public domain. Author: United States Armed Forces.

46 'Iraq war costs U.S. more than $2 trillion: study, published in *Reuters*, March 14, 2013.

47 The number will probably end up being higher even than that. Joseph Stiglitz's book on the topic *The Three Trillion Dollar War* gives, as the title suggests, a higher estimate.

48 'Exclusive: Cheney on global warming' published on *ABC News*,

February 23rd, 2007.

49 T. Flannery, *The Atmosphere of Hope*: Searching for Solutions to the Climate Crisis, Penguin 2015, pp. 134-5.

50 Quoted in 'The Nation He Built,' published on *Politico*, January 7th 2016.

51 P. Krugman, 'The Stimulus Tragedy', published in *The New York Times*, 20th February 2014.

52 Poll published on *IGM Forum*, February 15th 2012.

53 These estimates come from M. Grunwald, 'The Nation He Built', *Politico*, 7th January 2016.

54 Remarks of the President in Town Hall on HealthCare, Central High School, Grand Junction, Colorado, August 15th, 2009.

55 The phrase was coined by Sarah Palin who envisaged, falsely, a world where the government would decide whether elderly patients were worthy of care.

56 Subsequent Supreme Court challenges *National Federation of Independent Business v. Sibelius* and *King v. Burwell* have so far upheld the constitutionality of the law, with Chief Justice Roberts, a judge nominated by George W. Bush, breaking with expectation and supporting the law, a rare example of bipartisan thinking during the last years. For his pains, Robert is now a hate figure for the right.

57 This setback for Democrats has an interesting postscript. In 2013, Scott Brown in turn lost his seat to Elizabeth Warren, the current darling of the left and a possible vice-presidential pick for Clinton in 2016.

58 'The Billion Dollar Bank Heist', published in *Newsweek*, 11th July 2011.

59 Published on the US Government Accountability Office website, July 31st 2014.

60 Creative Commons Attribution 2.0 Generic license. Attribution: Arasmus Photo

61 Published in *The New York Times*, 26th July 2010.

62 On 9th February 2016, the Supreme Court voted 5-4 not to implement the plan until all legal challenges are heard.

63 M. Grunwald, 'The Nation He Built', *Politico*, 7th January 2016.

64 Remarks by the President in Address to the Nation on the End of Combat Operations in Iraq, August 31 2010.

65 2016 State of the Union Address.

66 Remarks by President Barack Obama at Fort Bragg, December 14th 2011.

67 These statistics come from 'Monthly Updates on the Covert War', published on *thebureauinvestigates.com*, 2nd February 2015. The figure a year on as I write this is no doubt higher – and will be higher still by the time the reader is reading this.

68 J. Goldberg, 'The Obama Doctrine', published in the April 2016 issue of *The Atlantic*.

69 Quoted in R. Yassin-Kassab and L. Al-Shami, *Burning Country: Syrians in Revolution and War*, Pluto Press, 2015.

70 This work is in the public domain in the United States because it is a work prepared by an officer or employee of the United States Government as part of that person's official duties under the terms of Title 17, Chapter 1, Section 105 of the US Code. Author: Voice of America News: Scott Bob report from Azaz, Syria.

71 This image is a work of a United States Department of State employee, taken or made as part of that person's official

duties. As a work of the U.S. federal government, the image is in the public domain per 17 U.S.C. § 101 and § 105 and the Department Copyright Information.

72 This phrase also comes from the Goldberg interview. I sometimes wonder whether Obama really enjoys foreign policy: 'shit show', 'don't do stupid shit'. It makes him reach for cloacal language.

73 'American deaths in terrorism v. gun violence in one graph', published on *CNN.com*, December 30th 2015.

74 A. Deaton, *The Great Escape: Health, Wealth, and the Origins of Inequality*, Princeton University Press, 2015, p. 212.

75 *https://www.whitehouse.gov/the-press-office/2016/05/01/remarks-president-white-house-correspondents-dinner*.

76 *Preservation News*, Volume 20, Number 8.

77 This can be watched at the following link: *https://www.youtube.com/watch?v=jhw69ihw4nk*.

78 Interview with John Dickerson on *Face the Nation*, 24 January 2016.

79 T. O'Brien, 'What's he really worth?' published in *The New York Times*, October 23rd 2005.

80 Quoted in 'Trump is Exaggerating his Net Worth (by 100%) in Presidential Bid', *Forbes.com*, 16th June 2015.

81 Trump can be seen making this claim at the following link: *https://www.youtube.com/watch?v=6rNWNg9z1bE*.

82 Quoted in 'Trump is Exaggerating his Net Worth (by 100%) in Presidential Bid, *Forbes.com*, 16th June 2015.

83 Under Creative Commons Licence 2.0. Author: Michael Vadon.

84 President Barack Obama, 'Why We Must Rethink Solitary Confinement,' published by *The Washington Post*, 25th January 2016.

85 Quoted in M. Tomasky, 'Can He Be Stopped?' published in the April 2016 edition of *The New Republic*.

86 R. Lizza, 'The Dual Face-Off', published in *The New Yorker*, 2nd January, 2016.

87 D. Axelrod, 'The Obama Theory of Trump', published in *The New York Times*, 25th January 2016.

88 A. Roberts, 'Donald Trump is the Mussolini of America with Double the Vulgarity,' published in *The Daily Telegraph*, 31st January 2016.

89 *http://www.mediaite.com/tv/trump-defends-ban-on-muslims-no-different-from-how-fdr-treated-japanese/*

90 J. Bouie, 'Donald Trump is a Fascist', published in *Slate*, November 2015.

91 'Bill Maher Prevails Over Donald Trump Lawsuit By Sitting and Waiting for the Donald to Figure Out to Drop It Himself', published on *lawlandblog.com*, April 9th 2013.

92 The full skit can be watched at the following link: *https://www.youtube.com/watch?v=um-qDHu2kOI.*

93 U. Eco, 'Ur-Fascism', published in *The New York Review of Books*, June 22 1995.

94 Quoted in C. Campbell, 'Fox News issues incredible response to Donald Trump's Twitter poll about going to the Fox debate', *uk.businessinsider.com*, published on January 26th, 2016.

95 G. Thrush, 'Obama on Iowa, Clinton, Sanders and 2016',

published on *Politico*, 25th January 2016.

96 C. Dickens, *The Pickwick Papers*, published in 1836, Heron Books. p. 190.

97 This United States Congress image is in the public domain. This may be because it is an official Congressional portrait, because it was taken by an employee of the Congress as part of that person's official duties, or because it has been released into the public domain and posted on the official websites of a member of Congress. As a work of the U.S. federal government, the image is in the public domain. Author: Frank Fey (U.S. Senate Photographic Studio).

98 'Is Ted Cruz Really an Awful, Terrible Jerk?' published on *Mother Jones*, 25th January 2016.

99 Speech on the Senate floor, November 20th 2014.

100 E. Collins, 'Cruz stands by calling Obama sponsor of terrorism,' published on *Politico*, 29th July 2015.

101 'Bob Dole Warns of 'Cataclysmic' Losses With Ted Cruz, and Says Donald Trump Would Do Better', published in *The New York Times*, January 20th 2016.

102 Letter to John Wise in Francis N. Thorpe, ed "A Letter from Jefferson on the Political Parties, 1798," *American Historical Review v.3#3 (April 1898)* pp 488–89.

103 Cohen, Marty, David Karol, Hans Noel and John Zaller,. *The Party Decides: Presidential Nominations Before and After Reform*. Chicago: University of Chicago Press, 2008.

104 'The Families Funding the 2016 election,' published in *The New York Times*, October 10th 2015.

105 Quoted in 'Where the 2016 Republican candidates stand on climate change,' *CBS News*, September 1st, 2015.

106 Quoted by Michael Tomasky in, 'Hey Middle Class, Hillary Gets It,' published on *The Daily Beast*, 14th July 2015.

107 'Rubio flips on amnesty and flops,' published on *www.lifezette. com*.

108 The results of the most recent poll can be found on: *http://www. gallup.com/poll/187922/clinton-admired-woman-record-20th-time. aspx*.

109 *Vox* reported on January 26th 2016 that among the candidates Hillary Clinton was recognised by 97% of the population, just ahead of Trump on 96%.

110 T. Harnden, 'Hillary Clinton's Bosnia Sniper Story Exposed,' published in *The Daily Telegraph*, 25th March 2008.

111 Not that Sullivan is in any way an apologist for Clinton. He recently had an anti-Hillary fit on the Bill Maher Show: 'Has she ever given a speech that you were inspired by? Has she got any good retail skills? Is she able to come across on TV?'

112 C. Hitchens, 'The Case Against Hillary Clinton,' published in *Slate*, January 2008.

113 This work is in the public domain in the United States because it is a work prepared by an officer or employee of the United States Government as part of that person's official duties under the terms of Title 17, Chapter 1, Section 105 of the US Code. Author: Presidential file.

114 This image is a work of a United States Department of State employee, taken or made as part of that person's official duties. As a work of the U.S. federal government, the image is in the public domain per 17 U.S.C. § 101 and § 105 and the Department Copyright Information. Author: Department of State.

115 H. Clinton, *Living History*, Headline, 2003, p. 69.

116 For many she hasn't always got it right. Ashley Williams recently interrupted Hillary Clinton at a private South Carolina fundraiser to protest that Clinton had once advocated bringing black children "to heel".

117 This statistic is quoted on the organisation's website: *www.vitalvoices.org/what-we-do*.

118 K. Brower, *The Residence: Inside the Private World of the White House*, Harper, 2015, quoted in 'The Secret Lives of Hillary and Bill in the White House, published in *Politico*, April 7th 2015.

119 This is taken from the Issues page of Hillary Clinton's campaign website: *www.hillaryclinton.com*.

120 H. Clinton, 'How I'd reign in Wall Street', published in *The New York Times*, 12th July 2015.

121 M. Tomasky, 'Hey Middle Class, Hillary Gets It,' published on *The Daily Beast*, 14th July 2014.

122 The link here is: *www.hillaryclinton.com/issues/climate/*.

123 *http://www.state.gov/secretar/20092013clinton/rm/2009a/11/131713.htm*.

124 W.B Yeats, 'The Second Coming' in *The Poems*, Everyman, 1990, p. 235.

125 G. Thrush, 'Obama on Iowa, Clinton, Sanders and 2016', published on *Politico*, 25th January 2016.

126 J. Stiglitz, *The Price of Inequality*, 2nd edition, published in 2013, p. xiii.

127 'Why I'm voting for Trump', published on *CNN.com*, 27th January 2016.

128 'Trends in the Distribution of Household Income between 1979

and 2007, published by the Congressional Budget Office, October 25th 2011.

129 Quoted in 'This election could be the birth of a Trump-Sanders constituency,' published in *Vox*, 30th January 2016.
130 L. Fang, 'Where Have All the Lobbyists Gone?' published in *The Nation*, February 10th 2014.

131 Quoted in *http://althouse.blogspot.co.uk/2008/06/what-did-bob-dylan-say-about-barack.html*, June 8th 2008.

132 This file is licensed under the Creative Commons Attribution-Share Alike 3.0 Unported license. Attribution: Gage Skidmore.

133 Quoted in B. Stone, 'Bernie Sanders Campaign Totalled $33 Million In Campaign Donations In Fourth Quarter Of 2015,' published in *International Business Times*, 1st February 2016.

134 P. Dreier and P. Clavel, 'What Kind of Mayor was Bernie Sanders?' published in *The Nation*, June 2nd 2015.

135 Z. Jilani, 'Bernie Gets It Done', published on *alternet.org*, October 17th 2015.

136 H. Clinton, What President Obama's Legacy Means to Me, published in *The Huffington Post*, January 19th 2016.

137 Sanders' patchy record on gun control is likely a reason that Black Lives Matter haven't warmed to him more.

138 Throughout the primary season, Clinton won a large proportion of the over 65 vote including by 39 points in Missouri and 54 points in Ohio. See A. Chozick, 'Older Voters May Be Hillary Clinton's Answer to Bernie Sanders' Youth Appeal published in *The New York Times* on March 20th 2016.

139 This file is a work of a United States federal court, taken or made as part of that person's official duties. As a work of the United States Federal Government, the file is in the public

domain in the United States. Author: Steve Petteway, photographer, Supreme Court of the United States.

140 In this analysis I have relied on a superb scholarly article published on March 9th 2016 the *SCOTUS blog* by Michael Gerhardt 'Getting the Senate's responsibilities on Supreme Court nominations right'.

141 Remarks made by President Obama Announcing Judge Merrick Garland as his Nominee for the Supreme Court, March 16 2016.

142 Public Domain as product of the United States Federal Government, Executive Branch, The White House, Executive Office of the President of the United States. Author: White House.

143 There is nothing new under the sun: there is mention of the virtues of hybrid government in Aristotle, and John Calvin also wrote of the virtues of 'checks and balances'.

144 Quoted in Tindall/Shi *America*, Fifth Edition, 1993. For a full discussion of separation of powers see pp. 224-7.

145 Figures quoted in C. Cillizza, 'Democrats are winning the Supreme Court fight over Merrick Garland. Big time' published in *The Washington Post*, April 19th 2016.

146 Quoted in Amanda Taub, 'The rise of American authoritarianism,' published in *Vox*, March 1st 2016.

147 C. Dickens, *Little Dorrit*, Book 1, Chapter 10, 1855-7.

148 J.M. Coetzee, *Diary of a Bad Year*, Vintage, 2008, p. 15.

149 Thomas Hobbes, *Leviathan*, 1651, from Chapter XIII, 'Of the Natural Condition of Mankind As Concerning Their Felicity and Misery, 9.

150 K. Williams, 'Our Hobbesian Left', published in The National Review, October 9th 2013.